Tolstoy in Riyadh

King Saud University Men's College,
Daraiyah, Saudi Arabai, 1984.
Photo by Debajyoti Aichbhaumik.

Tolstoy in Riyadh

A Story of a Teacher and Her Muse

Chris Cryer

2011 · FITHIAN PRESS, MCKINLEYVILLE, CALIFORNIA

Portions of this book were previously published in *Damazine*.

Cover photograph © copyright by Lesley Daley, www.photolesley.com

Published by Fithian Press
A division of Daniel and Daniel, Publishers, Inc.
Post Office Box 2790
McKinleyville, CA 95519
www.danielpublishing.com

Distributed by SCB Distributors (800) 729-6423

LIBRARY OF CONGRESS CATALOGING-IN-PUBLICATION DATA
Cryer, Chris.
 Tolstoy in Riyadh : a story of a teacher and her muse / by Chris Cryer.
    p. cm.
 Includes bibliographical references and index.
 ISBN 978-1-56474-517-0 (pbk. : alk. paper)
 1. Cryer, Chris. 2. Women teachers—Biography. 3. Tolstoy, Leo, graf, 1828–1910—Influence. 4. Americans—Saudi Arabia. 5. Mothers and sons—Saudi Arabia. 6. Saudi Arabia—Biography. 7. Riyadh (Saudi Arabia)—Social life and customs. I. Title.
 PS3603.R95T65 2011
 814'.6—dc22
 [B]
           2011018082

To Carol Lee, who charged me with two tasks—
to serve Montessori and to write about it.

Acknowledgements

This book is the product of much collaboration. Thanks, Lowell Foster, for talking me through the early chapters when I feared my own style. Thanks, Judy Garthwaite, for reading the manuscript the way only a true friend can read a true friend, with personal connection and shared emotion. Thanks, Dee Volz, for always being my mentor in writing, showing me how to live inch by inch the work we do. Thanks, Narayan Sengupta, our one friend left in our lives from Riyadh, for helping bring this story back to life and sharing it with us still.

Author's Note

I beg your patience with the following conceit. Though Tolstoy was never in Riyadh, I brought him there and sustained his presence for myself because I knew he had already experienced what I was about to go through. Tolstoy and I have the same kind of favorite place. Mine is Arabia; his is Chechnya. Both are Islamic cultures with an old-world lifestyle. We love these places for themselves and not for the fruits of our dealings with them. We're not diplomats, politicians, or businessmen, just people who'd as soon spend the evening with the locals as anyone in the world.

We were both radically changed by our experiences in these environments. Tolstoy lifted himself up from the dissipated first half of his life to the second inspired half with Chechnya as his watershed period. Chechnya became his touchstone to test life back home for its real value. He lived two lives, the one before, and the one after Chechnya. His favorite of his last works, *Hadji Murad*, was about Chechnya, and he sought at the end of his life to escape his home, heading, many feel, for Chechnya.

In this commonality Tolstoy is my best friend. We were touched by similar people in an equally important way. Hence, he is my big brother on the topic of this journey and a big enough brother to lend real clout to my study of a desert world little recognized for its richness and dignity.

Contents

Some—liberals and aesthetes—consider me to be mad or weak-minded like Gogol; others—revolutionaries and radicals—consider me to be a mystic and a man who talks too much; the officials consider me to be a malicious revolutionary; the orthodox consider me to be a devil.

I confess that it is hard for me.... And therefore, please, regard me as a kind Mohammedan, and all will be fine.

—Leo Tolstoy
from a letter written at his estate,
Yasnaya Polyana, in April 1884

Introduction

IN THE EARLY 1980s I accepted a one-year contract to teach at King Saud University in Riyadh, Saudi Arabia. A friend suggested that I apply there because times were hard in Alabama, where I was a divorced single mother, owning a small Montessori preschool in an environment in which I was ill-equipped to deal with business bureaucracies and sometimes vicious competition. My days were charmed, but we were frankly a poor family.

There was an international surge of professionals pouring into Saudi Arabia at the time, and the country was as wealthy as it has ever been or is likely to ever be. It was in the early stages of the kind of development we've recently seen in Dubai. All this convinced my friend to encourage me, but had only slight influence, actually, on my final decision to go.

Something else clinched my decision that proved to be fortuitous. My fourteen-year-old son added point blank that he *wanted to go*. I was amazed to know that then, as I am amazed today to know that he has over the years become a professor of international labor, writing for a legal encyclopedia on North Korean trade agreements, multi-lingual in Asian languages, with a strong memory of those years in Saudi Arabia when he learned to speak his first foreign language—fluent *Hijazi* Arabic.

We did not know that we'd become international people, and we owe these motions toward breadth of language, culture, belief, and spirit to the Saudis. Those I met in Riyadh did something unforgettable for me that I wish we would all stop and do for each other. In their unique, Bedouin way, they took me in when I needed it most, as if I were a waif crying in the desert. Like the famed hospitable Bedouins of yore, they offered me everything they had, including deep friendship, all based upon the miraculous assumption that I had some inherent value to be shared and celebrated.

That anyone in this pre- or post-millennium can make way and time for such acts continues to astound me. I found my worth there and thank the Saudis for being the wise parents who raised me through my second adolescence. I've become, in essence, a special blend—by nature American and at heart Saudi.

We've been through hard times together since the 1980s. The Saudis have shrunken their vast wealth for some of the saddest reasons. Our two countries seem both more closely allied and still more afraid of each other than ever. September 11, 2001 caused us to view each other with apprehension. Acts of terrorism in both countries and wars mutually involving us add a serious, confusing, and unsettling element to Saudi-American relations. Next, oil scarcity and Middle Eastern unrest have us once again shaking hands more nervously than ever.

I treasure my memories of life in Riyadh preceding this tension and see some value in reflecting in the simple way I do here in terms of person-to-person experiences that opened doors in those days. It's refreshing to remember the people then over the issues now. Writing this account of Saudian experiences renews my sense of that past. Even better, it helps lift some of the heavy veils that have obstructed our sense of each other since then, at least long enough to think new again, the way I could and did in 1983.

A note on the role of Tolstoy in this journal is called for. These days I teach college literature in California, with Tolstoy flowing through the In and Out boxes on my desk. He acts as a filter for my thinking in many areas, particularly regarding cultural and moral perspectives in classical "western" literature. In *Tolstoy in Riyadh*, Tolstoy is an old friend returned to help walk me through the attic of Riyadh memories. Until now, I found myself unable to share and record this story. Most people in my life in the U.S. do not share my views of this part of the world. Once I decided a Riyadh review can be as much about Tolstoy as about me, I felt I could travel in delicate spaces less alone.

Tolstoy loved the Chechen Muslims and experienced great disappointment in his attempts to rally his family to do sociological work and camp among them in the Caucasus. I've tried rallying my family back with me to Riyadh with the same result. In my imagination, Tolstoy is the one person most *available* for this return trip. So I asked him, and as I read over my work, I see that he really has come, in fact with some gusto and depth.

I am also sincere in wondering how Tolstoy would have experienced and recorded the Riyadh I knew. Stopping to imagine and add my assumptions of his perspectives undoubtedly challenges me and enriches this work. He is an arresting companion to take to any setting.

Part One

Dhahran

IT'S A ZANY IMAGE, the idea of Tolstoy in Riyadh, the old or the young Tolstoy, either way, belligerent and scowling, haunting the dusty streets, checking the action, sniffing out the vendors rank from their spicy meats, who are always sitting without budging, always too liberated to listen to his anarchical rhetoric, never needing his penitent spirit of conversion, or caring, as he might for them, to own greater parcels of Riyadh's desiccated floor.

I carry Tolstoy with me to Riyadh, not really of course, but in the voice of my pen that wants to take him everywhere, since he alone can speak to a place properly. My pen is old and clogged with Tolstoy ink. I'm just wishing he were still here to explain, better than Lawrence, better than Asad, what everybody's doing in the Arab world that keeps them wobbling like Sterno in a sea of long, uneasy flame.

Fourteen hours after JFK, I feel the soft air of Arabia. The airport in Dhahran is immaculate and cool. It's unlike the Riyadh airport later, hellish with hawkers yelling out corporate names to catch the polyglot new employees, exhausted and accepting, unable to understand their company cards on sticks. In Riyadh the transport curb is always thick with drivers for women and executive pools of expatriate men that begin to look like cattle, badly dressed, that is suited, which is unsuitable in Riyadh.

Life itself in the capital is more exciting than in Dhahran. Soon to be, in Riyadh, things will be hopping—palaces popping out from hillsides, signs to Mecca, armed guards poised at gated embassies, and wrapped women here and there tucked into corners so as not to greet strangers like me. Riyadh is a capital of tradition and strength, like Jamestown, Washington D.C., and Valley Forge in one. We come to live it that way day by day the same way American oil workers live in Dhahran, in the humor that it spouts. Dhahran spouts nothing but oil and then stores it. There you sense hard work and hard sleep, and that is all. It's the home of ARAMCO, but you are not to know it. ARAMCO is a *hidden* city.

It's Dhahran Airport, my first stop, that now fixates visions in my mind. We arrive during Hajj and it is transcendent. It is the people, the men, the Hajjis themselves. Though they should be going or coming, they seem stopped, finished, completed in the moment; so filled, so spoken, they are now almost silent in the white Saudian light. Everyone waits in a white draped sheet, standing in lines under a spent and late-day sun that sprays the entire room of glass in its pale, white dusk. It is the whitest moment I have ever known, a white that seems to warm and ground the Hajjis. But they know about it and I do not.

Tolstoy *knows* these Hajjis, and I wish I did. For me they're in a hum, but he knows what they're saying to each other and why. I need some dialogue badly, when an agent approaches me gently, scooping up the moment with sweeping arms that give the stairway to me, the entire stairway into a small and shiny Saudia jet. "Madame, you should go in now, before these men." "Oh, I am not alone. This is my son here." I tell him that I know how to travel. I am a lady, albeit born in the West. He lifts my bag, and is so inviting, I want to follow. "You must both go now, before the men."

I try to count these men. Can this be right? There are hundreds, fully shaven and washed for prayer, humming and fingering their beads, looking less like men of the desert than like yogis from

India. But we are required to go before them, so my son and I
ascend. It seems a long ascent. They do not see my ankles; I hold
my skirts in close. We leave the sea of white below, as the sweeping
walls of glass enshrine the Hajjis like a hub of orchids in a garden.
They are not commuters, travelers, or businessmen, but some kind
of Meccan hosts. If Meccan were a language, they speak it now, and
it's different. I have not been closer to Mecca yet.

Could Tolstoy know so soon, sooner than I, what the Hajjis
think and say? My pen says:

One short dark man wants to show his family pictures to
another, twenty years younger but distantly related.
   "This is little Khadija," he tells him.
   Khadija's eyes are radiant and her hair shiny, long and
black. She's clearly his favorite child.
   "Ahmad, she has a bike, only two wheels."
   "No. She's so young. Three? Where can she ride it?"
   "She rides it inside," he says, "all around the house."
   "Not in the kitchen?"
   "Well, it's okay with me, but her mother says no. Not in
the bedrooms either, of course. They're carpeted."
   Ahmed takes out his own small things from inside his
swaddling clothes. They must be religious souvenirs. I can't
tell what they are.
   "Hmm," croons the older man. "Will you keep that one
or give it to your wife?"
   Ahmad reaches inside again with difficulty and retrieves
more.
   "This one is for you," he says to the older man.... "No,
keep it."

Then they resume their steady drone, which fades into a Hajji hum,
and my son and I see no more from our ascendance to the door to

greater Arabia. The older man and Ahmad know what thing it is they shared. I don't know anything about it, but I see and I wonder. There is a soft feeling to this place. It's agreeable, quiet, and white. Night begins to drain the glow. Finally, adjusted, tucked, belted, and pillowed, we fly.

Riyadh

RIYADH IS THE cosmopolitan place. Expatriates are pulled here from major centers of the world, and ninety percent are foreigners enslaved to bosses who first hold their passports and second offer water, the liquid that made *Wahhabis* famous in the grand and revolutionary democratization of wells. Some countries nationalized industry, but the Riyadh royals nationalized water, knowing they had the one place in the world where water is gold. The resting place of princes and the counting house of Mecca seem enough for a place to be about.

Mere minutes out of our cushy jet, we stand next to the Riyadh Airport sign, dazed by throngs we'd all expect in Old Calcutta but not in this elegant, newly built city of kings. The scene at the local transport curb looks less like a dispersal center than a riot. Though Saudi Arabia is likely the only country that has never allowed or even dared experience a public riot, crowds of agitated men are all shouting at the same time in a variety of languages. They look sweaty and concerned like true radicals until I'm able to focus on the signs they're carrying. These are actually just drivers for the immense mass of incoming workers! I've seen corporate greeters all over the world, but never on such a scale.

I finally see *my* corporate card on a stick, "King Saud University," and gesticulate as women will who are drowning. It's the sea of humanity I'm drowning in. "Sir, Sir! Wait. They're searching my bags." Behind me on an endless conveyor belt that receives and never returns materials, my *foreign* literature is being swiftly abandoned, confiscated by security guards for the tasteless things it says and the Hollywood beauties *Time* magazine shows, mostly in ads. My first reaction is to scream until I note the faces of my fellow travelers, arms crossed and eyes glazed in acceptance, all patiently holding their frustration at bay. I can't talk to the guards, so I talk to myself. Okay, I'm free of it, really, travel magazines and a few recent novels; if they will only spare my tiny collection of Tolstoy. Tolstoy, more my companion than I can ever explain to those who allow no idols at all, is in severe crisis, dangling on the edge of the conveyor, overlooking a floor of sticky, mangled, paper garbage.

Can I live without him if they take him? Will they understand and honor his dying words—"What must I do now?" Will they see him as I do, not as a distraction but as a centering force, the most mature of *maharam*s (escorts for ladies), a cross between the most protective brother and the wisest grandfather? Not really, because they throw him on the floor. I actually step on my own Xeroxed copy of "Master and Man," before I realize it's not just another piece of security-trash.

"Can I keep this one?" It sounds like a question, but the truth is, I'm getting back on the plane if the belted guard says no. In fact, he's lost interest in my question and the whole trash heap. He's holding the nastier materials in a special bin and seems to consider my floor pile like chicken feathers at a barbeque. I scoop and run, stuff myself into the KSU jeep, and sit as tightly as I can. I try to reflect that *my stuff* at this point is *my stuff* or I'm going home.

Then we start to rumble over unpaved, rocky hills, and my fourteen-year-old just loves it. This jeep trip sets his first reaction to Riyadh on a positive note. At the end of the year I'll be advising him that "You can't go home again" when he realizes his nights cruising with young adults in BMWs are over. His salaried buddies will regularly make the rounds of juice bars together after work till eleven or twelve at night, schmoozing their way through balmy, starlit cafes. He has only ten months before returning to Alabama, where fourteen-year-olds are confined to riding their bikes down the block for a Slurpee. It's as though someone had given him the keys to a Harley-Davidson and said, "Son, there's no need to ride with your parents in Riyadh." We bump and fly over what seems like boulders, and everything hits the air except the rest of my books, which I stuff underneath my body and stretch over to hold down.

The guest house is glorious after a day and a half of travel. Our room is full of soaps, chocolates, and whispering servants. It even comes with a charming man from Austria, who is quiet too and never says that we are not married, which the servants, we come to find, assume we are. When I look a second time, he is gone. He must have actually trudged patiently to the housekeeper's quarters with this fact, because it's the middle of the night, and suddenly he's gone. The cohabiting of unmarried persons is certainly unheard of in Riyadh and could affect our continuation of contracts, not to mention upsetting our reputations from the start. I'm sure he deemed it best not to even say goodbye, as we simply do not see him again. We had to part once the truth was discovered, and he sits now just a lovely ghost in my memory. Riyadh seems a place of dreams, including that one.

Marc and I are, despite everything, in the mood of a marathon slumber party. The longer we stay up, the livelier we get. In spite of ourselves, it finally seems that day one has come to an end. I have the sense that we are singing one great song, played on an old breaking-down Victrola. We gradually notice that everything around us is silent, every room in the guest house as well as the vacant space left by the Austrian. The servants have disappeared too, and there is no buzz of cars at all outside. We can't see anything out there because our windows are narrow and designed to meet the ceiling instead of people. It hits us, as well, that we've also lost all sense of time, even of the day (fourteen hours ahead), Thursday starting the weekend here instead of Saturday. Even the annual calendar bears no resemblance to the Gregorian. We are well beyond jet lag, and trying to separate cultural impressions from pure exhaustion.

Just as time shifts us from one scenario into the start of another, deciding that we are the only ones still awake in the city, my son looks up to the street-lighted sky outside our window to announce what looks like dawn. We chomp on chocolates and smell our soaps, wallow in the linens, and consider the significance of the question, the significance of day one passing and the arrival of day two.

But there's a sound. It draws us out of bed. It comes from the windows, so we look up again. My son gets onto the desk chair, the desk, and finally the top of an armoire. I follow him and we scrunch there half-sprawled, staring into the empty streets. There's a thread of light on the horizon, and we just look hard. There is nothing to see. But we still hear it and freeze to hear it well. The *Adhan*. It's the *Adhan*, the call to prayer. We know about it but never stopped to think that we would hear it ourselves, at dawn, like this, right now. We don't budge till it's over.

The *Adhan* needs to be described, but is indescribable. It is not just song, or prayer, or culture. I have heard some say it is annoying. Others complain about one voice versus another. I've known people who especially attend the call to prayer in certain neighborhoods famous for their muezzins. But it is not a fashion or competition. Really, it is always the same, one voice calling all voices. My son says nothing about it, climbing down and into bed, declaring only, "It *is* dawn."

I didn't know what to say either, but feel the *Adhan* is something Tolstoy knew. For his Eastern Orthodox moments of sacrament, candles, and incense, for the funerals and births he's described of circling friends, repeating their desperate, begging prayers from deep within their souls, he knew about the *Adhan*. He knew the Chechens and he knew their *Adhan* to be a stirring and important reverential cry. In his novella, *Hadji Murad*, his Chechen characters find,

> …With that the song ended, and at the last words sung to a mournful air, [a] vigorous voice joined in with a loud shout of "Lya-il-lyakha-il-Allakh!"… Then all was quiet again except for the… whistling of the nightingales from the garden.…

I remember that, climb down and into bed. It's hard to sleep. I want more than ever to know where I am and what is happening around me.

Daraiyah

The Most Expensive Campus in History

DARAIYAH IS SOMETHING to see. This Riyadh neighborhood is a legend for me, coming from Montgomery, Alabama. It is one vast university community, constructed alongside the famous '80s project that also included an all-new King Saud University built by the Blount Brothers Construction Company from Montgomery itself. People at home knew about it because Blount was exceedingly proud of its contract to erect (at the time) the most expensive university ever constructed. They held lectures for the public in Montgomery to share the Blount story, which was a fascinating one. One point they made about their own Riyadhian adventure had to do with the trials of translation, not just Arabic-English and English-Arabic but culture-to-culture and custom-to-custom.

It seems that a few years after initiating the KSU building project, a devastating fact became known to the brothers Blount. Mega-millions of dollars and labor hours later, after sending architects, engineers, and managers to Riyadh for years of intense effort and collaboration, after drawing up so many complex blueprints that unique buildings were designed just to contain *them* properly—there was a sudden realization of impasse. It seems that when translators moved in to certify planning, they were unable to approve the project. The problem was simply translation.

The interpreters claimed that the paper trail so far was untranslatable, and consequently meaningless as a joint Saudi-American venture. All construction stopped, while Saudis and Americans tried painstakingly to understand each other. Will it take me years like the developers just to find out I have no idea what to expect or what I'm doing here? At the time my contract was signed, the Blount Brothers were barely beginning to climb out of culture shock. They initiated further years of translation/negotiation (they claim it took that long) similar to the stop-and-start babble we see in TV coverage of U.N. hearings.

Home
The sense of the word "oasis" comes to mind when I recall the effect of my first sighting of Daraiyah, rising out of the desert in all its modern convenience. It's half an hour outside Riyadh along the smoothest road we've traveled. The highway itself carves the only unnatural imprint upon the sands, until the Blount buildings emerge, a monumental hospital, set high on a hill, and the construction site and completed housing complex below.

That hospital, atop a ridge of high sands, has a haunting effect on me, a monolithic eye institute built on a scale one hopes will never fill with patients that sits in an overseeing manner to warn of the wiles of the swirling sands. Every time in the future, as I come and go from Daraiyah, I am forced to look up at the eye hospital, aflame at night in gaudy green and gold lights, and think how dangerous the sands must be that Saudis need so much care for eyes. It always makes me worry about the limitations of my sunglasses. I promise myself to stop everything and cover my face if swirling sands move in upon us, as sometimes they do. Riding from town to Daraiyah, a suburb with no suburban setting whatsoever, we always see several mini-sandstorms, moving like tiny tornados.

But arrival is always good, and on our first encounter, thirst-quenching and particularly inviting. Most of the employees assigned apartments in Daraiyah also know of its fame, have requested it, or are otherwise feeling fortunate to be there. Hearsay has it, however, that medical personnel for the so-called "Shangri-La" hospital have even better quarters in town near the old hospitals while waiting for Blount to complete their new site here.

On first sight the community looks ancient, a walled city whipped by winds and sand with buildings unseen huddled behind for shelter. In fact, Daraiyah proves modern, immaculate, and green inside its ancient-looking façade. Sixty percent of the community is courtyard, meticulously maintained round the clock by Yemeni workers in orange uniforms. They tend all growing things as if it's their personal nursery. If you mention a wilting plant, they whistle for a troop of specialists with prop sticks and sprays. It is intended to be a complete community and has a mosque, of course, a grocery, housing offices, a preschool, an indoor pool, a men's restaurant, a women's restaurant, and other amenities I never fully discover.

By the time our KSU jeep pulls up at university housing on the Blount site, there are actually new completed apartments for several hundred faculty families, one beaming general hospital not yet open, and a vast area of measured territory, empty, but squared-off and tagged for future construction. I feel like a spy from the Blount home office.

The apartments are spacious and built solidly, but even these newest of buildings are not like home. Walls are incredibly thick and ceilings high. The entrance to our two-bedroom unit is at least ten feet in height and double-doored in exquisite, varnished wood in honey patterns. Inside more orange-uniformed men insist we wait till they finish cleaning. Everything already looks perfect, but they scrub walls, polish wood, and shine chrome until they are satisfied.

We have lots of windows looking out on the courtyard, where Saudi and other families are walking their babies and strolling, but I never see any dogs. It is not Saudi tradition to house pets, presumably to compensate for a long history of Bedouin tent life embedded with camels and goats. Saudis sometimes reject dogs, in particular, as it is popular to follow loose *Hadith* (stories about the Prophet) that suggest canines are a health threat. More solid *Hadith* and the *Quran*, others say, stand by dogs more than Saudis will admit.

The university apartments prove spacious and uniquely so in one way that is for me Saudian. They have substantial formal halls. There is generally a front hall for receiving guests that leads to a long hall running behind the living and dining rooms, connecting the rest without exposure to the front. I am sure this is for the privacy of women from men. The KSU kitchens in Daraiyah, although the latest in design for 1982, still maintain tradition long lost in American kitchen design. They are completely separated from the living area and have back doors and windows to back porches. I feel this supports the cooking ways of women, who in most cultures, after all, like to haul in sizable kitchen supplies directly from the car and stay to socialize, right where they are, over their long-simmering pots.

We are finally alone in our splendorous quarters, and hungry. The problem is that I have almost no money left due to a sudden six-week extension in the contract schedule that caused me to spend my entire travel budget while waiting for the Saudi go-ahead before leaving Alabama. I'm not worried because KSU has promised an immediate stipend of half a month's salary for move-in costs upon arrival. It appears to be a weekend, but there is a grocery near our building, and I have the U.S. equivalent of eighteen dollars cash. This should be tight to get through the weekend, but enough if we rob our guest house welcome bag of all that's left.

We try the grocery but a scrawled bilingual sign says it's closed for the *Eid*. How long will the *Eid* holiday be? I know *that* isn't in my guidebook. We haven't met any neighbors yet, so we go back inside to check a phone directory that came with the phone.

Luckily, Daraiyah has a kind of resort atmosphere. All utilities are always on, all phones connected, and when we check the directory, we find we can call all community facilities on our line. Thank God (*Alhamdulillah!*), there's even a number for the Women's Restaurant, and it answers during the *Eid*. They deliver and will send over two large lunches immediately for twelve riyals. At this rate, I might make it through the weekend and into the payroll office before we starve. We supplement with our welcome bag, now down to chocolates, cookies, a few crackers, and some tea bags.

Shortly, men knock on our substantial front door and enter like bellhops from a Four Seasons hotel. They are wearing some kind of black servers' outfits and bend towards us ingratiatingly, place a small feast on our dining room table, and leave. We are fairly astounded again, but getting used to surprises. I still remember that meal in delicious detail, as I ordered exactly the same thing a few hundred times after that. Later, I worked in Daraiyah and ordered it for lunch every day: a small grilled meat with soft seasoned rice, fresh hummus, tabouleh, fresh flatbread, olives, and tea.

I go out several times that day and the next to wait for a bus into town. The bus stop has a bench with a roof for sun and schedules in Arabic and English, but no buses are coming. On the third day, I know we are in trouble. I have not yet been to that celebrated payroll office that looks like a grand mausoleum, and I need to find when, where, and how to do it right away. There is never anyone else waiting for a bus. I seem to be the only one who doesn't know what's going on. The housing office is right next to the bus stop, and it seems closed all this time too. This is not the kind of problem I want to use to introduce myself to my neighbors. In fact, I've never borrowed a penny from anyone and totally panic at the thought of doing it now. Even my colleagues are foreign (to me). Only a few are from the U.S. Most are from Europe and the Middle East.

Inadvertently, I notice movement in the housing office, or I think so. I swish over in my long skirts and try the door. It's unlocked, though the lights are not on, which seems unusual for offices. Inside I see a tall Saudi gentleman gliding around in his copious white *thobe*, moving from one file drawer to another.

"*Asalam alaikum*," I interrupt. (I know just a little Arabic, but not how to say excuse me.) "*Min fudluk*" (Please). I add an empty hand gesture, "Bus?" "*Alaikum sa-lam*," he answers. Then in perfect English he adds, "Are you looking for a bus? We're on *Eid* holiday and there won't be one for another ten days."

At this point my eyes well up with tears, and I automatically, with no aplomb whatsoever, blurt out "But, but, but..." between choking on my own fears. The housing official then reaches into his pocket without another word and pulls out one of those incredible huge wads of bills I eventually will become comfortable with in this land of Oz. "You can go to Payroll after the holidays," he says, "and pay me back then." He assures this will be no problem, and I assure that I live three doors from his office and can be relied upon. He's given us the equivalent of $1,500 cash!

If there is a single story in the U.S. of a stranger giving $1,500 to another off the street as an unsolicited and unrecorded loan, I think it should be noted. I have never heard of such a thing, though I sense that my experience is not extraordinary for Saudi Arabia. After that, we live high for the holidays, and I can afford it. This is the best job I've ever had.

In his wisdom, I am sure Tolstoy would, at this greedy moment in my career, rather than congratulating my wealth, remind again of Hadji Murad, the stoic and virtuous Chechen chieftain he wrote the novella by that name to honor. In fact, Murad, a true historical figure, also crossed cultures and faced an interminable wait upon doing so. Murad, after his family is taken hostage by a rival chieftain, has no choice despite his skill and fame, but to turn himself over to the Russian enemies to share secrets in a trade for Russian help to save his family. His entire story is about waiting for that help. The question is can he cross cultures successfully when it is called for? Will the second culture deliver? His Chechen culture was warm, but the Russian culture cool.

Sadly, Hadji's story is a tragedy. Crossing over to the Russians proves to be disempowering. He cannot wait long enough for the military, the tsar, and the bureaucracy to learn to trust and work with him. He feels forced to go it alone, and in his final and independent attempt to storm the stronghold that will not release his family, loses his life. He unfortunately moves from the warm culture to the cool one, and the cool one simply cannot deliver.

The Russians and the Americans I know believe in "every man for himself." Like Murad, I have much to wait for, hope for, learn, and try. Hadji failed in the cold culture, without the warm connections I am now experiencing for the first time: a tight culture with built-in support, a sense of implied honor, and personal trust. *Alhamdulillah!*

The Desert

Quiet.

DARAIYAH IS QUIET, even in summer. Sounds are different and truer. We have no TV and only know one person (expatriate) who does. That means rhythms familiar to my own head are no longer dancing around me. The screaming and moaning of football has been muffled to death. Jingles for inane products are finally wiped out of my memory. The various unfamiliar voices that always hung out in a corner of the living room are gone. And it's all right.

Amazingly, our single green courtyard rarely chugs with mowers charging and recharging. The brain-frying road static from cars is so far beyond our gargantuan compound walls that I can't detect it even when I try. There's no slapping and re-slapping of tires on asphalt. Our museum-thick building knows no one on the other side. I can see the desert, but I'm walled off from it. I'm in the mirage we've all read about in *A Thousand and One Arabian Nights*, green, abundant, and feeling surprisingly tented and tended.

Sometime later I meet a longer-settled colleague who has a TV, only to discover why no one else does. There's mainly *one* subject on TV day and night, seven days a week, and that's the King. We see him signing edicts (that would have to be the right word), boarding flights, receiving dignitaries, even eating and stiffly partying in swishy, Jesus-style wide-armed robes, in opalescent white *thobes* that always cover his sandals and leave you wondering what his feet look like. The TV (and the newspaper for that matter) are King-based and King-controlled and never record him washing up (even for *Salat*), recreating, in sports, or doing anything else that could help us identify.

What we know about Britain's Prince Charles we will never know about King Fahd. Clearly, he is not trying to identify through TV. He's governing by TV, and there's something at least halfway democratic about documenting every public thing he does, though commentary is sadly unthinkable.

It is good to know what one's King is doing, and if you are unable to watch his governance at home, you can always check with anybody for that kind of common knowledge. There are few ads that I can remember anywhere; no billboards or TV sales, just a few, much appreciated, unintentionally humorous newspaper ads. All this lack of advertising seems an invitation to think.

One Japanese employee Marc and I always remember from our entry at the Riyadh Airport was dismissed immediately as a sort of misfit (we feel) because he insisted on wearing a dark suit, thin tie, and shiny black shoes for the ten days he lasted. Had he made it through attire orientation, he might have discovered his rather serious crime. For a week and a half he was the only uncomfortable man in Saudi Arabia, a real threat to generations of "peace and tranquility." As he returned to Tokyo, he shared with us his pain to have to return, not to uncomfortable clothes, but to commercialism and all its in-your-face modernity.

I accept the quiet well and think about Marc at the Howeedys'. His first experience is such a grounded one. Professor Howeedy came from the U.S. South like us and traveled with his wife and son on the same route. They also just arrived and live in our building. But Dr. Howeedy is a close advisor to the president of the college, a scholar, and established academic. I feel more like a common insect that just woke from a long sleep and crawled out from under a big rock into the sun. While I'm thankful for some quiet in which to gather my sense of impressions, as a Muslim-American VIP, Howeedy's already deeply comfortable in Quranic study with not only his own son, but mine!

This seems like fabulous luck. Marc's steady, daily, gentle moments of Islamic discussion over tea and baklava seem better to me than a symposium of lectures by some of Said's hopefully now refuted, long-dead Orientalists like Burton, Philby, and Doughty. There's surely nothing more Saudi Marc could do than study the *Quran* with a scholar at home.

Marc's a reader. Now with his portable library cruelly limited to three hard covers and a comic calendar, he still comes with a lot more Saudi savvy than I ever hoped to have. It already seems I'll never catch up with him. At JFK he insisted I change into long skirt and sleeves and a wide and proper scarf in order to make an elegant debut Saudi-side. By now, he can probably suggest the same with the full support of Quranic justification.

Privacy

Riyadh is a capital city, but in its many feudal, thick-walled corners, it can also be quiet and amazingly private. All I can hear right now are distant voices, talking, laughing, and then trailing off. This muted aura is changing me faster than anything, because it stares at my life and asks me what I'm doing. I resist answering myself, but I can't stop the fact that it changes something. It's easier to think here and there's a lot to think about.

Ryadhians move so often in clumps. Whole families of women travel with their servants around town, each group in a van. Sedans are rare because of this need to pack a group at once. But they also know where to go to be alone and are simultaneously masters in the art of creating separateness and privacy. I see from my window a gaggle of boys moving fast and shapelessly like a cloud of white *thobe* silently blown far away. Then their whirl of white disappears, and they're gone. Boys universally know how to be alone, but Marc and Khalid will spend every weeknight now in Howeedy's dining room pouring over Quranic issues. They are the academic boys, the good boys, the family men. They're the expatriates (two percent) that blend in.

Like the Antebellum South

Even in town the homes are quiet by night. They are high-walled and gated with the windows off the courtyards closed. It reminds me of New Orleans, where I was raised, of the backstreets in the French Quarter where people are quiet too, if only by day. The intimate enclosures, each unique, provoke a sense of secrets for the outsider, while encasing the closed traditions of the insiders the way thick church exteriors exaggerate and protect their sanctuaries.

Expatriate men always ask me about the women there, because they are rarely introduced directly to Saudi females. In public places, Saudi women are trained to stay together in private cliques, clasping their black silks over and around them, every tiny wisp of curl tucked obediently into their scarves. On the other hand, I see very few with covered faces (*niqab*) and those mostly piling out of the biggest and dustiest vans, suggesting some difference between urban and outback culture.

Saudi women remind me of the Southern belles of antebellum Dixie. Everyone knows Mitchell's Scarlett O'Hara in *Gone With the Wind*. She is to Southern scholar McIntosh-Byrd a metaphor for the South itself, who:

> …must clothe herself in femininity in the way that she literally clothes herself—a physical and mental distortion of natural form designed to create the illusion of an ideal.
>
> In doing so, her character calls into question not just the

performative aspects of femininity, but also the performative aspects of a culture that demands such ritualistic self-
preservation in order to function.[1]

Hubert H. McAlexander says[2] of Mitchell and her portrait of our
own Southern U.S. gentility that she "takes pains to show the spine
of a Southern matriarchy underlying a patriarchy." Such women
(the "cared for" women ensconced in unsolicited privacies and
honor) are by no means unimportant just because they're pack-
aged to the side. They're actually given exaggerated importance, as
any current American androgynous person can see. While we are
increasingly unsure what's masculine and what's feminine in any
category, Saudis cling to their women symbolically, holding on to
their distinctiveness as proof of the significance of family in all its
traditional customs and roles.

These pretty, rarified women do become my friends over time,
their dusty streets disguising a maze of queen bees behind doors,
ladies who do not answer their doorbells, but brew teas, bake
sweets, and serve ongoing mega-meals at leisure twenty-four/
seven.

Back in Montgomery, I tutored Saudi men (from Maxwell AFB
War College) and their wives in their homes for years, eating my
way through each day, unable to insult anyone's *mezza*. I carried
simbouza home, guzzled saffron rices with chicken dripping in
golden broth, wrapped up extra cinnamoned squares with almond
slices on top, and grew to prefer lamb minted, tea minted, and any
meal graced with mint, feta cheese, or Kalamata olives.

I know, as they sing in the musical *South Pacific*, that "I'm only a
cockeyed optimist," that I can be counted on in Pollyanna fashion
to find what I love and need as I open to loving and as I find myself

1. In "Gone With the Wind (Criticism)," Answers.com
2. In "Gone With the Wind," *New Georgia Encyclopedia.*

in need. This is undoubtedly mindless of me in the presence of always so many bright people who know better. I suppose that after years of marginal pay at home, an indifferent family, and frustrating pilgrimages from one church "community" to another, offering my son no Sunday school classes of any greater merit than our local Episcopal "Purple Pickle Tree" curriculum (which we never could define, decode, or even decide to care about)...I suppose that after all of that, I might have been refreshed by Zen in Japan, or I might have gone to Russia and embraced Tolstoy's Orthodoxy in its beatific design, with icons eyeing me, candles for sacredness, and incense for calm. I might have done these things, but they might have left me right where my own culture did, alone. Only in Saudi Arabia do I feel quieter and less alone at the same time.

Here We Are on the Moon

I move outside alone and toward Howeedy's to get Marc, when I spot my first colleague. We must be colleagues, two thirtyish American-looking women, rigged to cover head and foot with wimpy scarves and no *abayas* (women's cloaks), with hair sticking out at every opportunity, not quite covering our necks, naked faces pathetically pale in the garden lights, no jewelry and no perfume! We look so practical, like two Puritans trying to skirt around the Casbah in the dark.

She speaks first: "Well, here we are on the moon." I never forget this line. It's so apt, opens so many conversations. The expanse of sand we are starting to call home looks exactly like a moonscape and feels as a moonscape must, vacant, unenterprising, and empty enough to absorb sounds and activity, even plans and confidence. Commercialism and competition as we'd known them seem insufficiently hardy here, barely able to breathe in a landscape so inhospitable to contrivance.

She is right. We are on a moon, one with a commanding sense of its own destiny and will. We are slowed by our long skirts, quieted by thick walls, and arrested by a forbidding wilderness. Best is, it makes me giddy, especially at night, when, in fact, the whole world really comes alive in Saudi Arabia.

"Wow! It *is* like the moon," I answered, "and it's great out here tonight. Where are you from?" We are, we find, of course, ESL teachers, from the States, and a little earlier for the semester than we expected.

"C'mon tomorrow," she says. "We're taking the bus to the Al Khozama (Hotel)."

"It's running?"

"Thank God, yes." She's as thrilled as I am.

Of course I have to go and especially in our own little clump of "badly-*hijabed*" women. Tomorrow, our buses will run for the first time since the *Eid*. I'll pour like a Saudi woman out of a huge muddy vehicle in a mass of females. I know where to borrow money if I need some, and I can get advice from a son who's becoming an expert on "The Book That Makes All Things Clear."

Part Two

Our Women and
Their Women _____

He in his madness prays for storms, and
dreams that storms will bring him peace.
  —Tolstoy

HOWEEDY PROVED TO BE the soothsayer from *Julius Caesar.*
He did not poke into my nicely settling dream to say, "Beware the Ides of March." He just prepped us appropriately for what was to come. Thanks to his Saudi-style introduction and grounding, regular subsidized dining from the Women's Restaurant, "fireside" Quranic chats, and an uncle-ish personal loan from an elder in the housing department, I knew already when I boarded the university women's bus that I had crossed into the badlands.

I should have preceded the crowd and been the only unmarried, thirty-year-old American female employee in Saudi Arabia. I should've come earlier like T.E. Lawrence, the noted British militarist and diplomat, a masochist who could thrive on less, exquisitely exhilarated by testing his mettle against discomfort, thirst, and animal bedding. Simplicity was his god, and he came to passionately love the Arabs. If I'd come with the right identification, I could've returned to the U.S. Congress after Saudi Arabia the way Lawrence returned to Parliament, sweaty, angry, proud, and demanding in a roar fair relations with the Arabs.

Instead, I board a bus of hussies, wheedlers, and manipulators whose inner hearts are easily read. They wear what singles us out, feigning ignorance and innocence, scarves resting barely on puffed coiffures as Bhutto always did in Pakistan, long straight skirts with deep slits that accent rather than relax the silhouette and lead the eye to peek, and striking cloth patterns made for the eyes at runways. We fill up three quarters of the bus with the cutest assortment of "alternative *hijab*" ever seen. I find my eyes casing the complex quickly, hoping neither the Howeedys nor my benefactor from the housing office are out and about.

Most striking in our group is a Texan who clearly has been an authentic beauty contestant. Though she's dressed like a British detective, it's hard to take your eyes off her. She was born to be looked at, with light blue eyes like stars and skin that glows. Her body does not respond to the controlling force of *hijab*. She's buttoned into a knee-length khaki trench coat with a wide belt and buckle. Her long-legged pants emerge, somehow, still too stunning for the street. Her hair is the fatal blond that cannot be masked even when no single strand escapes her scarf.

Blondness is a dangerous commodity on the streets, and I'm not going to ask if she knows or not. Eventually, I have two blond friends, but never the courage to embarrass either of them by bringing up the subject. Over time I come to sit with the Texan in adjacent offices at work every day, and she finds me attractive enough to double-date with (she *always* has options though no one else can dream of them). This liaison, however, requires that she give me advice. I really should use nail polish and work on my nails more, and if I do not begin wearing tight clothes under a raincoat immediately, I'll leave this country a blimp. She's figured out that loose flowing long gowns are an obesity trap.

Our odd assortment rolls into town, where we get out a mile from the Al Khozama. At the entrance, the guarding rows of doormen instantly break down. Generally, more than half of us are showing some part of our necks, which we can get away with, but which does not give us the casual anonymity of sensible natives who have easier access and movement. If some of your neck is showing and there's an essence of blondness, however hidden, in your group, more than the usual doors will be opened for you.

Fawning of the service staff begins. I say "No thank you" a lot. As we enter the echoing marble emporium and break a near dead silence I've wished for in some libraries, it's as if everything we're saying is being broadcast over a speaker phone. Thus we smirk and giggle our way around the Al Khozama. I'm not sure what the actual effect on the public is, because I'm afraid to give eye contact to any Saudis, aware the whole time that not seeing them does not mean they're not seeing me.

Despite the fascinating interpretations of clothes coverings that we represent, none of us is in an *abaya,* the pretty and amazingly effective, silk flowing cover-up that's expected. Saudi *abayas* are always black, and it's clear that color is the element of taste we are least able to part with. We not only wear colors but bright colors, and not only giggle, but are loud and personal. I occasionally see some kind of African women in Riyadh who also wear bright colors and grab the eye, but they are neither voluptuous nor loud. Also, I sense the Africans fear what I fear, that a single eye, lifted for the singlest second, will nonetheless be caught in a dual engagement of consequence.

I cannot remember the eating part in the restaurant, only that before I leave, four in my coterie have set dates with waiters. At this beyond illegal act, I leap from my chair, saying that I have to meet Marc at a nearby bus stop, and flee to the gift shop to reregulate my breathing. I am able to buy a fabulous English-Arabic dictionary and a Saudi cookbook, and run on silent feet, eyes on the ground, to the bus stop. Marc is there, holding a taxi to the Women's College, where I hope to gather back (moving-in) pay, and answers to where he can go to school.

Word has it, eventually, that these English teachers thumbed their way back to Daraiyah that day. That is the last time I accompany my colleagues anywhere far from the women's bus. I am ready for work, Marc's school, and to meet some *Saudis*!

Tolstoy's Dialogue Between the Women and the Patriarchy

If we take a worldwide vote on codes of behavior for women in public, my colleagues will win immediately and easily. But Wahhabi tradition fashions a different custom, much challenged but not yet altered. My colleagues' stance extends to the college where they take on the establishment directly, which fires back with incredible memos, such as those accusing female faculty of "standing around the exterior of the college" and "wearing lipstick and make-up." Just what these ladies challenge in the academic program I am either unable or unwilling to sort out above the din of quarrelsome meetings in which factions, alignments, and excessive emotion are the order of the day.

Over time a Gestapo fear develops in the community, as men and women are plucked out of the faculty one by one, their "crimes" not usually clear to me, as we live increasingly amid the exaggerations of gossip coupled with the reality that expatriate instructors are regularly being deported with as little as three days' notice. Whether the victims are men or women, it's often over relations between the two that issues arise. Clearly, the testiness at academic meetings is derived from an original distaste with being told how to live what expatriates consider their *personal lives*.

Here is the rub. One culture's personal matter is another culture's public issue. The more religious and integrated a culture is, the more personal matters are public issues. Who can deny human rights? Then again, when does freedom become license? What makes a secure and wholesome society anyway, more freedom or more decorum?

Tolstoy lived on the moral fringe of an elite class so decadent that it was violently brought down soon after his death in the Revolution of 1917. He, I know, infused his characters with the moral confusion and distress he hoped would bring them closer to the decorum side of the argument. His three female figures, Anna Karenina, Masha from "Family Happiness," and Marie from "Father Sergius," alone dramatize nineteenth-century turmoil Tolstoy decries between males, who wish to wrap their women in a safety of respect, and the women, who want to test their feminine wiles.

Standing in the middle of the same raging conflict in Riyadh, likely at any moment to be labeled dangerous by either side, I thumb through my texts and pull out some epic Tolstoyan dialogue on the subject, in this case, between the young Masha and her much older husband, Sergei. Their argument is painful, each reaching desperately to understand and respect the other; yet we sense there can be no resolution. It seems the role of women was and will be a question for the ages and a matter of angst throughout time. To be in Riyadh as an expatriate is to live this argument.

I imagine Masha representing the expatriate women and Sergei the patriarchal head of Wahhabi custom and law:

"Why do you suppose that I can never help you in anything?"

"Not help me!" he said, dropping his pen. "Why, I believe that without you I could not live. You not only help me in everything I do, but you do it yourself. You are very wide of the mark," he said, and laughed. "My life depends on you. I am pleased with things only because you are there, because I need you..."

"Yes, I know; I am a delightful child who must be humored and kept quiet," I said in a voice that astonished him, so that he looked up as if this was a new experience; "but I don't want to be quiet and calm; that is more in your line, and too much in your line," I added.

"Well," he began quickly, interrupting me and evidently afraid to let me continue, "when I tell you the facts, I should like to know your opinion."

"I don't want to hear them now," I answered. "I don't want to play at life," I said, "but to live as you do yourself. I want to share your life, to…," but I could not go on—his face showed such deep distress. He was silent for a moment.

"But what part of my life do you not share?" he asked; "Is it because I, and not you, have to bother with the inspector and with laborers?"

"That's not the only thing," I said.

"For God's sake try to understand me, my dear!" he cried. "I know that excitement is always painful; I have learned from the experience of life. I love you and I can't but wish to save you from excitement. My life consists of my love for you; so you should not make life impossible for me."

"You are always in the right," I said without looking at him.

"Masha, what is the matter?" he asked. "The question is not which of us is in the right—not at all—but rather, what grievance have you against me? Take time before you answer, and tell me all that is in your mind. You are dissatisfied with me: and you are no doubt right; but let me understand what I have done wrong."

But how could I put my feeling into words? That I again stood before him like a child, that I could do nothing without his understanding and foreseeing it—all this increased my agitiation.

"I have no complaint to make of you," I said; "I am merely bored and want not to be bored. But you say that it can't be helped, and, as always, you are right."

"Masha," he began in a low, troubled voice. "This is no mere trifle; the happiness of our lives is at stake. Please hear me out without answering. Why do you wish to torment me?"

"Oh, I know you will turn out to be right. Words are useless; of course you are right." I spoke coldly.

"If you only knew what you are doing!" he said, and his voice shook.

I burst out crying and felt relieved. He sat down beside me and said nothing. I felt sorry for him, ashamed of myself, and annoyed at what I had done. At last I looked up and saw his eyes: they were fixed on me with a tender, gentle expression that seemed to ask for pardon. I caught his hand and said, "Forgive me! I don't know myself what I have been saying."

"But I do; and you spoke the truth."

The truth for Tolstoy is that this discussion is a projection of his own marital trauma from which he escaped in secrecy and silence just before dawn on October 28, 1910. He rode out of his life on his favorite horse at age eighty-two with no goodbyes and no notification. Word is he was headed for Muslim Chechnya.

The truth for me is I now know I'm in the wrong group. Threatened by this tease-and-fire dialogue is my vision of meditating Hajjis, my wondrous thick desert walls, my pretend uncle, the studious Howeedys, and the new silence I'd never heard before.

My Escort

Urban Excursion

OUR TAXI RIDE fulfills all the worst-heard fears and tales. My taxi vocabulary is limited largely to *yassar, yamin,* and *alatul,* left, right, and straight ahead. I say (but still can't spell) "*Collea al Binet*" (Women's College), and after a thirty-five-minute version of a reputedly ten-minute trip, the driver stops where there is no sign in Arabic or English. He jerks the brakes and we cough in a dust cloud and wipe the sweat off the place where our hands are gripping shiny faux leather seats.

"*La, la*! (No) *Collea!...al Binet!*"

He's adamant: "*Aiwa...hene*" (Yes...here).

The merciless spot he's chosen to abandon us in has no trappings whatsoever of a college for men, women, or monkeys for that matter. There is no campus, gate, no students, only wildly glaring sun fixed meanly over a long stretch of seedy wall violated by irregular weeds, in charge, stretching menacingly out of Georgia clay-colored mud.

An odd assortment of men squatting near and leaning against the wall finally comes into focus for me. So I ask them in the same pidgin Arabic for help, to an astounding murmur of consensus. This *is* the Women's College. At this, our driver ousts Marc behind me and peels off backward as if we won't notice. I peer into a narrow opening in the wall, leaving Marc to blend into the all-male foreground that has come to be our best indication that women's studies is somewhere nearby, somewhere behind.

Wordlessly, we get it, that Marc will have to challenge the same sun that turned these likely drivers of students into leathery thin prunes of men. They have an air of having sat there all their lives, enjoying the leisure of living on-call, mired in dry dirt and blinding glare. I promise Marc to return with the first water I can find and enter into the vast façade of walls.

I fall first into a deliciously dark earthen corridor. The shade alone is incredibly inviting, and a very old man seated on something low and ottoman-like is greeting me and offering…I can't believe it…a drag on his huge water pipe. It appears the whole bubbly contraption is a staple of life at his webby guard post.

"Yes, of course. *Min fudluk*" (Thank you). I'm looking for water, but this becomes a champagne moment for me. My eyes meet the old man's in watery bliss, as if we'd drunk all night and day together. This sweet, wet, fruity mash, *arak*, remains the flavor of Riyadh for me. One deep draw opens my mind to peer around, to find the educational "meal" on the menu for which the appetizer has been set. Elsewhere I'd have hugged the wrinkled, bony doorman, but here I know to cast my skirts politely forth. This *is* the Women's College, after all, or at least it's supposed to be.

The lumping of flat pueblo-like structures in the maze that follows does not invite with its on and off outdoor walkways and occasional stubble of wild twigs. It's not Dorothy's Yellow Brick Road trimmed in homey touches on one side and threatening horrors on the other. It's not quite Alice's Wonderland either, despite the frustrating reality that there are no building signs in any language and that the doorman reminds me of Carroll's Caterpillar, who along Alice's way sits on a toadstool smoking a hookah. He's the one who restores her from miniature size back to her original self. Speak of same, I begin to feel better inside the walls of the *collea* and detect a small library to my right. No dazed Alice, I'm right this time, and the smell of books and the sight of a room full of stacked shelves is the most reassuring sight since home, and there are people on hand in the back. I see no English titles, but find from here on an end to mazes and a-mazes, and finally the answers I came to get.

Manhood

Before I withdraw from the underworld of the Women's College, I receive the move-in stipend needed to repay my Daraiyah bene-factor, choose medical students over sociology or business majors, collect first-day class plans, and am devastated by one piece of shocking news. Marc will not be able to attend school in Saudi Arabia. My contract allots 8000 riyals for the education of the first child, and I'd assumed that would be enough. The actual cost of the American School is 16,000 riyals, more than I can possibly afford. I decide not to tell him *yet*.

Outside on the road something looks different. I look for Marc standing where I left him. I have his cup of water in my hand, but no one is standing now. How long was I in there? Where would he go? Suddenly, I detect his warm voice, his empathetic habit of repeating others' words, his tone, deeper this summer than last winter, the voice of a fourteen-year-old who thinks he's seventeen. While searching frenetically way down the street, I trip on his foot. He's not down the street. He's at my feet. He's squatting and squint-ing with the crowd and repeating short Arabic phrases as if they are familiar. My words run ahead of me, "Marc, what—?" while his eyelids drop in a signal of adolescent despair. *(Mom, be polite.)* "Oh. *Asalam alaikum*." I smile at everybody.

Is this my son, squatting for no reason in two loafers that look like grounded pontoons, chaffing deep-wrinkled pants now riding close to his knee? He looks as though I could tip him like a dumb cow. He and his colleagues, like castaways who have never known life with chairs, are engrossed, really engrossed in pidgin language.

Here we are without a ride home in the mid-afternoon heat, full of terrible news he doesn't know yet, and he'd like me to wait for him to close an unintelligible chat. They talk on dramatically. There's a lot of gesturing, grunting, and my favorite, spitting.

Worse. No! They're actually smoking, all of them. Marc and the others act like Bogie in *Casablanca*, flattening their cigarettes between thumb and finger, holding them not lightly but in a serious pinch. They purse their lips and exhale like the French, meditatively, as if it warms the brain. I should not be here, but I have no place to go. I have half a mind to hide out inside the *collea* until this is over, when Marc finally gets up, stomps out his butt, and makes his farewells. We walk first and talk later.

"There're taxis not far from here around the corner," he says, and, "Don't take this too hard, Mom. I don't smoke. It's a 'when in Rome' thing."

"What was that stuff anyway?" (I'd better know.)

"Beedis, some kind of Indian cigarette."

"I'm glad you don't smoke, but you *squat*?"

"I don't squat either. Hey, I know what we should do though. There's a shop right over there that's supposed to have cheap *thobes* and sandals."

We ride home with *thobes*, sandals, and an *abaya* for me, which feels right. Marc continues to claim that he is neither a squatter nor a smoker, but wait till he finds out how changed his life is, that he's not even going to be a student anymore.

Turnabout

Daraiyah's like a cool cave to a hot bear after our day on the road. I seem to be the first to start hopping taxis. None of my Daraiyah bus colleagues has a son or the issues that Marc and I face together. The public buses separate males and females, and we're not ready to travel that way yet.

Sitting with tea in the half-shade on our divan we can watch everyone come and go from their buses. All transportation is regular and free: vans for nurses, a mini-bus for my group, shopping trams for women, and school buses for kids whose parents clearly have tenure and higher salaries than I do.

We perk up at four o'clock to see the first-day batch of high school teenagers spill out of transport and into the courtyard. You can see every expression in the bright sunlight. They're laughing and lollygagging, as my Irish father would say, and one peculiar habit they share puts me on my feet and Marc on his. Several boys are carrying their books on their heads. I know some remote tribal people do that, but 1980s high school students from the American School?

Marc, already in his *thobe* with new sandals parked at the door, seizes the best books of ours to juggle himself, adding another every time he makes it all the way across the room. This is painful, so I sit him down and tell him our latest tough reality; he won't be going to school at all. There's an empty feeling in the air. It's suddenly apparent that we brought a mere four books for each of us and that all eight of them, now staring at us from the coffee table, amount to nothing. They do not a curriculum make. Sprawled ecstatically yesterday, they now look more like eight postage stamps without envelopes or anyplace to go. At this point I'd like to bronze all of his and put them on a shelf in memory of his past the way mothers bronze baby shoes that have no purpose anymore.

If we don't count the *Dungeons and Dragons* game books, the Matt Groening *Akbar and Jeff Calendar*, two Norton Anthologies, a few Tolstoy and other short works copied, the only thing left to grow on is the *Harbrace College Handbook*. "Okay, Marc, I've got it. You can spend the next nine months acing the *Harbrace College Handbook*. You'll be glad you did. It's the secret of success." He's smart enough not to reply at all. Later, cleaning up from dinner, he casually mentions how important it is to balance sciences, math, foreign language, and social science with English mechanics. Right, but we have seen almost no books in English and those at exorbitant prices in hotel shops. In my entire tour of duty in

Saudi Arabia I only make it once to the Women's Public Library, so great is the distance, the transport, and so troubling the absence of signs on streets, not to mention not being able to read Arabic signs at all. Mail-ordering texts is probably cost-prohibitive too. We'll need help even to self-educate. If no one knows what to do here, maybe we can send for a home schooling kit from the U.S.

While Marc's at Howeedy's I sit in the early moonlight at the bus stop and wait for the next shopping tram. There's an Islamic moon, a crescent and one star. I hope for something as beautiful on earth as in the sky and wait to ask the next driver if he goes near the Women's Public Library, where we might find a selection of books in English. The bus pulls up with no riders, so I have a good opportunity to get some advice.

"*Asalam alaikum*, do you go anywhere near the Women's Library?" I have one last moment of optimism.

"You the lady with the young man?"

"Oh, you know my son? He's fourteen. We're going into town tomorrow. It's the last day before school starts."

"No men."

"He's not a man. He's just my son."

"No. He's a man and we don't take any."

"Wait a minute. You mean he can't ride into town?"

"Not on this bus."

"Which one can he ride?"

"There aren't any men's buses from Daraiyah, sorry." He says this with complete finality, then closes his quiet accordion-style door and leaves me alone in the night, silent and depressed. This means for Marc an impossible combination, utterly no school and very little travel anywhere.

Instead of going inside, I sit right down on the bus stop bench and try to promise myself I'll think of something before getting back up. The night is beautiful. The desert is solid. My heart is in it. Marc's at Howeedy's doing the worthy thing as usual. He *deserves* a chance. I see a shooting star right in the sky over the housing office, and notice there's a little action there. The situation's the same as the night I ran out of money and met Mr. Al Mani there before.

I pick up my skirts and move quickly. It's already after eight. I can see it's Al Mani from the stairwell and find myself acting the same as the last time. I'm breathy, heart pounding, and need to get a lot of frustration off my chest.

"*Asalam*, Mr. Al Mani." He nods in a short bow. "You know, my son is incarcerated in Daraiyah. I cannot get him into school, and now I see he can't even leave on any buses at all." I should have made chitchat, but the moment had come when whoever I saw next was going to hear these words.

"Is he fourteen? Didn't you know? You have a *maharam*. You can move into town any time you want to."

"*Maharam?*" It sounds like something good, but?

"You have an escort. Single women live here and families. With a *maharam* you're a family. Families have the choice to live here or in town."

Oh my God! Everyone I know except the Howeedys is single. They're all wishing they even *knew* anyone in town. I have just received the news everybody dreams of. Marc will be beyond happy. This also makes him instant head of household, whatever that means. One thing at a time. There's only one more day before my school starts. Once we move and I start work, we can open our minds to finding maybe some other kind of school. A Muslim school would be fine with me, as long as they teach in English. Maybe there are other ways in the system to get an education.

I think of Tolstoy spurning all of his elite advantages as a youth in Russia. He found the army dissipating and was totally bored with law school. He wrote just for relief from the angst of it all, and *that* was his real beginning. Who knows what we can think of for Marc to do?

Pampered "Princess"

Wearing My Uniform

I THOUGHT I was the escort and now I'm the escorted. I'm an escortee and the only one I know or have ever known. In fact, I'm an escortee in an *abaya* and it seems painless to me, so far. The *abaya* is light and flowing, sleek, and a one-minute wardrobe solution. If you're off to the corner grocery and in blue jeans with stains and holes, you need an *abaya*. No one ever cares or knows what's under it. I could almost believe a nation of Saudi women's libbers, not yet out of the closet, had created it. Nothing is better for an ongoing dual existence. The Western raincoat cannot compare in ease, comfort, or style.

Escortees wear *abayas*, and I'm feeling particularly sincere about mine since I bought it before I ever dreamed that we would move into Riyadh permanently, where there are so many more places to wear it. Wrapped in mine, with Marc as escort, we leave Daraiyah with a mover in an open truck. Marc sits between us in the cab, fully in charge of the move, giving directions to our new apartment, holding a handful of papers regarding housing rules and utility payments. I do not open the doors of the pick-up or carry any items, however small, into our new home. Again, this is fine. I'm busy studying keys, sorting take-out *shawarma* and napkins, keeping uncapped tea hot, and meeting neighbors who warn

that there is more than *maharams*. We'll likely be followed when
we go about town.

I know my colleagues would bravely balk at the *maharam* idea.
At this moment a significant percentage are in offices protesting
all sorts of "conditions." Keeping up with these oral battles makes
up half of all faculty conversation. But I cannot help feeling quite
thrilled to move into the escorted group and to discover what's
there. Luckily, I have a first-rate escort. I do believe the trick is in
raising your sons well, especially here. Maybe Marc and I abide
in enough morality and self-esteem to take a cavalier look at any
government-backed "followers."

In town every woman has an escort. Any male of a certain age
(I never do determine what age) is sufficient. Most often he's a husband, and traditionally, Saudis marry early, adding to the supply
in terms of length of time spent with a husband-escort. Without
husbands, they make do, like me. I laugh to think of how many of
us have had to rely on older sons or younger brothers, much loved,
but not at all more reliable than ourselves.

Is there not, I consider, always more to do than drive in un-
driveable killer traffic (descriptive of Riyadh), handle bureaucratic
domestic tasks, open doors, and carry heavy objects? I'd rather
plan, shop, cook meals, decide what people should wear, and run
our social life. Do escort duties not add manliness we have rarely
achieved in our male children in America? Marc has taken to the
role like a duck to water and is on his own accord out getting directions to run our washing machine. This will be fun for me, but
of course, like everyone, it's perfectly private and secret who really
does what at home.

Western women have the right to do more, but that right often
translates into duty, and the duty into burden. People of some age
can remember when Americans felt women needed and appreciated "help with things." It's harder for us (as women) to *expect*
help from men (as men) today. On the other hand, male and fe-

male tasks seem to be melting into an androgynous whole based on nothing but practical need, and this is the most successful social change I've seen in my lifetime. It's great to see dads changing diapers.

Young women now, though, need to beware of choosing the most stressful multi-roled lifestyles, if we no longer have the old-fashioned support from a husband, brother, father, or someone else who can help in the ways men have helped women over the centuries. The psychological, physical, and monetary support men have given women in the past, if not irreplaceable, is certainly special and precious. If we are pregnant, nursing, or otherwise hormonally challenged, there are no longer protective perks for us set into custom. Since men don't have these challenges, we Western women may be equal in freedom but unequal in burden.

Over time I meet not a single woman in Riyadh from any country or culture who complains about her husband driving around on errands or handling price negotiations on expensive products. In fact, in our building I find a coterie of Western husband friends who do all the major house cleaning, too. As for moving around in public, we do it without men all the time, as do many Saudi women, though on foot, by bus, or with drivers. Expatriates keep warm all the stories about Saudi abuse they know, and we do hear about an occasional young girl unfairly espoused to an old man. Some teachers tell of female students who become pregnant and disappear. These for me remain tales, although I know such things and worse occur in all cultures; but there is no story I know that defames the tradition of men as escorts. We used to call them "gentlemen."

Tolstoy on Submission

Actually, I feel giddy about living downtown and trying out my new role. Oddly, giving in on the freedom to be my own spokesperson is opening doors. "Submission," I have learned, is synony-

mous with Islam. I know that Tolstoy's *Calendar of Wisdom* touts
the same:

> Just imagine that the purpose of your life is your happiness
> only—then life becomes a cruel and senseless thing. You
> have to embrace what the wisdom of humanity, your intel-
> lect, and your heart tell you: that the meaning of life is to
> serve the force that sent you into the world. Then life be-
> comes a constant joy.

It seems ridiculous to submit to a representative for myself, but for
me it will just be a convention. Saudi women submit to more than
most in the Arab world—for instance, the drivers' licenses they
are so uniquely forbidden. But there are other areas of submission more worthy of attention. Had Anna Karenina, Tolstoy's most
famous female character, submitted with great focus to some plan
or role, she might not have been a tragic figure. Clearly, Tolstoy
thought so.

Most of his characters wander fruitlessly though his thick works
stuck in their individuality and individual needs. Only a few win
out over the common psychology of their time and place. Levin,
the narrator in *Anna Karenina*, finds himself the hard way, learning to exult in his givens: fatherhood, country life, and field labor,
with no expectation of success or emotion. It's no longer what he
achieves or feels that counts. Focusing and believing in life make
him feel real. At the end of *Anna Karenina*, she is lying dead under
a train car, and Levin, far off in the country, is realizing his highest
satisfaction. She has given up on personal meaningfulness, and he
has found it outside himself.

For Tolstoy, submission is about the joy of work, the prospect
of losing oneself in constructive simplicity. He seems to fear least
those who love their work. Perhaps I will fear least women who
know their role.

Thoughts from *Anna Karenina* are taking on new dimension:

> The day and the strength had been dedicated to labor, and the labor was its reward. Who was the labor for? What would be its fruits? These were irrelevant and idle questions.
>
> Levin had often admired this kind of life, had often envied the people who live this kind of life...the idea occurred to him clearly for the first time that it depended on himself alone...to change....

My Saudis are so rich at this point in time that they don't work much at all. Every business and department has expatriate employees with only the executive director a Saudi. At home the Saudi women I know have more servants than any I've ever known. They do, however, remain busy and retain their ancient role, elegantly prepared for every day in scarves, perfumes, and heavy arms of gold, dressing always as women and not just as persons. They listen with the concentration of sages day and night to friends and family. They shell beans meditatively while servants speed-park their Mercedes. They bear long, three- and four-hour meals, holding state together as needed in this continuous cadence that is their life. They are there, as present as the gurus of India. Below their chandeliers, reliable, floor-bound, straight-up or leaning against walls, they sip uninterrupted tea and are the ultimate confidantes. The Saudi women I know hold social court every night for a lifetime, the same as American farmers who warm porch rockers at sunset.

The total focus of these grandes dames is on their family, friends, and guests, and these they attend with uncomplicated commitment. During my many years divorced and alone, not one American has ever helped find me a match, but Saudi women I know have found and are finding a husband for me right now. This is the generosity I need, a kind of collaboration I'd read about in

Tolstoy but never really seen. It's their generosity that sustains the Wahhabi ethic beyond what would seem to be its time, still supports kings, and follows, not clocks, but the call of the muezzin.

The escorted life *is* very different, both exciting and frightening, but for the moment I am just happy to be back in town.

Part Three

Riyadh Revisited

As If Man Could Fashion Time

Riyadh revisited sparks whole different parts of me. "How ya gonna keep 'em down on the farm, after they've seen Paree?" Moving from Daraiyah into the capital is like leaving a convent school for the debutante ball. The possibilities awaken a myriad of persons inside me. The variations in each day now seem endless.

The most exciting thing to spot in my neighborhood is no longer a small pack of camels and camel riders, though I'm thankful to leave Daraiyah knowing just a little more about that. I did learn from occasional observation of tiny tired-looking caravans that the *National Geographic* image of camel riders with faces covered but for the eyes proves true at times. Riders really do wrap their faces in *kuffiyas* (men's scarves). I've never had to use my scarf against the sand, but feel sure it's good to be prepared.

Now life is urban. There are the quiet informal mornings picking up *hubbs* (bread) for breakfast in the cool delicatessen cellars on our block, where some men, smiling but quiet, show up unshaven in their funny striped pajamas. There are the thronging over-packed buses full of bubbly teachers and friends on the five-minute lift to the *collea*. There are the luxurious closed up "siesta" afternoons that follow my eight-to-one, full-time workday. And in the end, there are the expansive evenings coursing the *souks* (outdoor markets), restaurants, hotels, and sometimes apartments of friends. There are even the camel races we never go to that seem popular only among Egyptian men, who follow every trendy European style and imitate Italians.

Special to Saudis and foreigners is the month of nights during Ramadan when the whole society, rested by a full day of meditation, emerges to stroll and claim the malls and cafes luxuriantly, with an enchanted air of evening picnic. The nights of Ramadan, in fact, move well past midnight, with little children falling asleep under halcyon skies. This great Ramadan calm sweeps across all the sands of Saudi Arabia to the entire Muslim world. Ramadan lights, like Christmas lights, glow late into even the least expected corners. Once they are out, another slow-developing day begins. Ramadan seems to set the model for the regular Saudian day. All Saudi days build quietly toward an active and exhausting night. Evening, in the desert, is always the true people time.

This time curve is thankfully perfect for me. Saudis stay up late, so they allow quiet in the morning, giving early work an air of non-importance. By one, when I am able to walk the two or so miles home, it is already time for shops to begin closing for the afternoon, which they do with cold finality, clanking down and solidly shuttering metal closures across the store fronts. This leaves no question that morning activity is really never meant to quite get off the ground. Then it's private time till *Maghrib* (sunset prayer), when neighbors rise, wash, pray, and begin the day that counts, doing business, not in a work mood, but in a social vein, shopping, insurance, business appointments, and students studying together. This order works because it builds up slowly, offers public time, private time, then social time and genuinely stops and restarts. I see no need to multitask or drone on. There is a time for everything.

The students study together at night too because Saudi students don't want to work alone. This old tribal sense is wonderful for stimulating interest in cooperative study but leads to epidemic confusion over whose work is whose. The two major issues at King Saud U. are control of what's considered cheating and deciding what's sufficient system testing. It's strange that in the U.S. we've been working to reduce testing and encourage cooperative learning among students, while the Saudis are pressing to increase testing and encourage independent learning. Saudi students are still trying to understand the difference between night and day. After carousing through their texts with friends all night, it seems uncomfortable for them to get up in the morning, go to school, and act like independent research scholars. If an assignment is completed, they care not by whom or how. It's natural to them to solicit the best talents they know.

In fact, my neighbor gave me a *Saudi Arabian Schools' English Pupil's Book* for first grade boys that I find fascinating. It not only introduces family- and neighbor-based lessons but international social perspectives, including recognizing and naming twenty British school boys, their school uniforms, currency, and flag, and of course, the art of polite money haggling, featuring seven-year-old Ahmed selling eight-year-old Saud a motorbike. Clearly, current and future monetary rewards of socializing are taught at an early age.

At any rate, the students, families, friends, and independent businessmen all thrive at night when the *true* Saudi day begins. It is possible, even likely, to find myself having to fit a lot of activities into one night. This means coordinating schedules, leading to a very long evening: starting at a restaurant, moving to a family gathering, cutting for a business appointment, breaking for a shopping pick-up, and ending in a few hours of garrulous group study. Just then, after ten, the phone will start to ring.

Riyadh is socially overwhelming for me, with more plans and meetings with more types of people than I have ever known, not to mention little notes, even boxes of chocolates, frequently left at my door. For the first time in my life, friends and associates are not suburbs away from each other but doors away, floors away, or at farthest a few streets away. The homesick expatriates need each other, and because they are without TVs, cars, movie theaters, and bars, they hang together more than ever.

The Sound of Salat

While the pace of Riyadh appears to be about social exchange and circumventing the sun, I'm forced to see it's also about two other forces, opposite forces that face each other like Cain and Abel. It's a miracle that neither has wiped the other out. Riyadh in 1982 proves to be almost entirely under building construction. It's also, as the bureaucratic seat of the Islamic world, almost entirely under meditative *de*construction five times every day, and has been since Mohammed's famous flight from Mecca to begin a new society in year 1 A.H. (After Hejira) or 622 C.E.

The builders are bold and loud, while the prayer rugs are rolled out delicately and silently and the pounding of shoes is laid to rest. The barefoot public, inside and on the streets, kneels and prostrates in soft murmurs of agreement. Eventually, each time, the thunder of machines also halts, and the peace of *Salat* wins again for however short a time. Both forces continuously interrupt the pace of business as usual, one as cacophony; the other as enforced quiet.

When we first approach Riyadh from the soft and sandy Bethlehem-style hills that sweep into it from Daraiyah, I am immediately struck by this strange symbiosis of construction and *Salat*. I hear the muezzins in staccato, begging for a quiet break, vying against the churning, metal-chopping of intransigent construction. Then I hear the quiet that intervenes for half an hour. This is the setting of our new home the day before school starts—a five-floor massive marble building that is being hosed down from roof to ground in a waterfall of bubbling silt and leafy debris. The air feels clean and fresh.

Making Home

Our apartment is amazingly spacious, even larger than the new
and trendy one in Daraiyah. It has all-marble floors, covered in
thick Oriental rugs, and three balconies for drying clothes. The
bathroom and kitchen have small circular drains in the middle of
the room for washing the floors, similar to what's being done in the
exterior halls. All these washing and drying techniques are new to
me, but I love this place and am ready to stay.

The couch is a huge art-deco velvet piece I'm ready to settle into
for homework. The long bedroom balconies seem romantic and
we have enormous armoires instead of bedroom closets. There's
even a separate dining room with a china cabinet. I cannot believe
this, because in my eccentricity, I've brought on the plane, over my
shoulder in a strong leather bag, a set of Wedgwood china for four,
each piece wrapped in a towel, including cups and saucers. It's the
most expensive thing I own, and I want it with me, even if that
means carrying delicate treasure on my arm and on my lap all the
way across the world. Next week, I'll buy a serious lamp and a large
plant (from Holland, like all plants in Riyadh), though they'll cost
hundreds each. I'm the only one I know who'll invest in decorat-
ing, but that's because I'm the one who wants to *stay*.

Sorting Mountains From Molehills

That same first day in Riyadh, hours before school orientation, I
slip out to a delicatessen on the side street behind our building,
only to have the grand opportunity of meeting Diane. She does not
seem like someone to meet. She is a disaster. I cannot believe my
eyes when I spot her, arms spread and voice hoarse with shouting.
The late day sun spotlights her on the otherwise shady street, looking like a brazen Kabuki warrior on stage. But no, she's holding a
one-woman protest against a Saudi bus driver! There are fifteen
or more riders and the driver watching as intently as I am, as she
stands hugging the front of the bus with her body, preventing it

from proceeding with her arms spread wide and her legs bowed in adamant fighter stance. She's insulting the driver loudly, non-stop, to an audience of nothing but silent amazement, including my own.

Finally, I decide I might save a life here. A picture flashes through my mind of those periodically publicly beheaded at a famous square somewhere in Riyadh I'd determined not to look for. She seems unlikely to stop ranting or to move her body out of the way of the bus. Her speech is amazingly articulate for what could be her last words. How well it'll be received in English, I'm not sure, but this is no time to think like a language teacher.

"Let those women into the front of the bus. This is not fair and not workable. How can they get change, tokens, directions? You've got to stop...."

She does not look likely to stop *herself*, so I jump right in as if we're old friends. "This is not a good idea. Stop right now. This bus has to go. Can't you see this is really dangerous? What are you doing?"

I think a Western audience on this quiet block is Diane's last expectation at the moment, because she stops calmly at my words as if this is a regular activity and the most amazing event right now is my arrival and involvement. I somewhat take over, guiding her to the curb and gesturing apologetically to the bus driver with the suggestion that everything's all right now and he can go.

"Wow! Are you okay? I don't think you should do anything like that. Whatever possessed you?"

"Well, it's just ridiculous, and they know it, and they ought to expect some trouble on this! I'm Diane. Who are you?"

"Gee, I'm Chris. I just moved into this building." I pointed up. "There's my window open up there on floor four."

"I'm on the roof. We have a penthouse, probably because I have a doctorate and I've been here two years. Nobody stays two years."

"Well, not if they feel the way you do."

"Hey, if you just moved in, I think I know your son. He's up-stairs right now asking my husband, Larry, how to use the washer. We have some ice cream, so come on up tonight."

"Ice cream? I didn't see any ice cream anywhere."

"The hotels have it, but I know one place."

I can't believe how important the washer and the ice cream are and how happenstance her protest is to her, but I am glad it's over and never really bring it up again, once I get a small lecture out of my system. "You really shouldn't protest these buses. It's extremely dangerous. You can't change things by yourself. Besides, I'm not sure how bad it is. Some women would rather not have to sit next to unfamiliar men anyway, and after all, it's free for women since there's no one in the back to make them pay."

"Those are the only good points," she says, still obviously actually more interested in ice cream.

Protesters are probably my favorite people in the world, and this incident gives me an immediate positive view of Diane. What protesters are like, though, I'm not truly sure. I had thought they're smarter than she's acting right now, but PhDs do have a mixed reputation. I think protesters may know a lot of interesting people.

This proves to be true. We have ice cream in the penthouse and Marc loves Diane, Larry and their entourage so much that he establishes something like dual residence. When he is not home, I assume he's there. Maybe Diane and Larry can think of something to do with Marc's unoccupied brain for the next nine months.

As for corporal punishment in Riyadh, I experience it as a topic of conversation and refuse to attend beheadings and make it real. I can talk about it as conversation but really do not want to participate. Somehow all the gossipers I know on this matter are men, who so love to gawk that I am not sure even one ever gave me an earnest, well-thought out reaction to the subject as a current Saudi issue. It's hard to separate their emotions from any logic they may harbor. They treat beheading the way my college roommates treated bullfighting in Mexico, as entertainment first and issue last.

I am enough a realist to note that, despite our casual proximity to the capital punishment public site, there are few beheadings at all, and Saudis register an almost negative crime rate, while guns and violence seem to mark badly both the reality and reputation of the U.S. Locking cars and doors is not a habit of Riyadhians. My mover-driver from Daraiyah, however, seemed above averagely crime deterred. When I lost a diamond ring from my finger in all the soapy housecleaning of the move and asked if he'd seen it, he turned pale with fright and never did relax around me again. He could not tell a request for help from an accusation.

Ice cream in Riyadh is special and it reminds me of home. As I come down the grand marble stairs from the rooftop, with the benevolent evening breeze descending behind me in the corridor that has no ceiling, I feel ready for school tomorrow, and after so many positive changes, ready for almost anything. On my floor, I hear my phone ringing. This is another first for us in the new apartment house. I manage to tear inside before the ringing stops.

But there is no talking on this call. Not from me. My brother Tim has died. Paralyzed in shock, I really cannot talk. I'm sorry I left Marc upstairs, because I need someone to respond, say something kind, and goodbye. I feel dead myself. In our family of four children, we had two teams. Tim was my team, not half of it, but to my mind *all* of it. Without him there is no team. I can't hold it up. He was a famous local lawyer in backwoods Louisiana, "ferocious in the courtroom," the obituary later records. He was my spokesman in all difficult matters in the family, the biggest of which was whether or not to work in Saudi Arabia. Tim was not only the only person in the family to back my plan, but the only person I knew to trust the Arabs.

Tim knew what I wanted and he was the only one. This is very hard, and I spend the rest of the evening finding a way to get to the international calling center to call my family back, to try to open up a little, to release and share some pain. University housing phones have free incoming service but no outgoing international service, and the international calling center charges a fifty-dollar minimum for outgoing calls. Two hours later at the calling center I share some numbed words on-line, but a tiny echo effect is playing all my words back to me while my family is talking, so that I realize I will get little out of the extravagance.

This truncated call seems a metaphor for what I expect to get out of my family in the future without Tim. I feel worse, and still worse the next day. I decide that I cannot teach my first day of school. In fact, not the second day either. On the third day, fully aware that life is rough and that we must all make our own way through it, I skip the busy trolley to the college and walk there slowly, enjoying the angry slap of one foot after another on the not so paved back route. I go, however late, to meet my first class at the Women's College.

The Women's College

Introductions

A T THE ENTRANCE this time there is no door guard with a hookah. He might be there somewhere, but the general presence of students and teachers in third-day mode is the greater reality. How is everybody so familiar with everything so soon? I find the Foreign Language Division and finally my class of pre-med girls. Unfortunately, communication here is worse than at the call center. When I start the introductory, get-acquainted material, they interrupt me.

"We're supposed to be on Chapter Four today. Can't you at least skip the syllabus and get on?"

Of course, I can do that. "You can read that at home. We can speed this up and be right on schedule in a day or two."

"You know," an unattractive and very serious young lady announces, "it's not fair that we missed two classes and have to take the same department tests as the other classes." She's clearly unforgiving.

"Girls, I'm truly sorry, but my brother died three days ago, and I am back as soon as I could make it. We should not have further problems."

"But, Ms. Cryer, you don't spell correctly either!"

What? At this point I realize it's a done deal that this class is destroyed. I don't spell correctly? There is no confidence between us. I look at the board and see under "Indications of Good Health" the word "color." Okay. That's it.

"Ladies, I see you are expecting British spelling. This is no issue. Which do you prefer? I can use either British or American." At this, I erase "color" and mark in "colour."

They are in no way happier. They have made up their minds. With me they will never pass their bi-monthly standardized tests given in a huge auditorium circled by severe-looking proctors and timed precisely to a loud and merciless buzzer. They look at me as if I am lying. They have no idea how Americans spell "color" but are sure that I am wrong.

At the end of this first class I head for the Medical English Office, where I discover that I am the only American in the department and that my boss is even angrier with me than my students are. We're teaching anatomy vocabulary, which admittedly I have never done and don't know in any detail. I've never been a science major and probably should have chosen to teach Business or Sociology students instead.

My boss, a huge imposing British woman with a large voice who, like my students, prefers to eliminate introductory politeness, furthers the case: "What's this I hear about your use of 'duodenal'?"

I have never had such a week for wordless response. She's right. I had to list the duodenum, but didn't really know it, am not sure about it now, and am looking for a place to hide.

"You young Americans come in here thinking you.... Anyway, do you have any experience teaching anatomy at all?"

The answer is, of course, no, but I'm not saying much lately. Eventually, I take myself to the Foreign Language Division head to try to decide what to do. First, I ask what the policy is for teaching varieties of English. Which English do they want us to teach, British or American? I am happy to teach either, but need to know which. Unfortunately, she merely looks at me quizzically, with the suggestion that this volatile subject will not be answered and is not even happily received.

Such is the Women's College. Like walking into a lot of walls. I soon find that the senior British instructors are long-time experts in Medical English with specializations in anatomy. I actually can understand how inappropriate I am for their department, so instead of bumping into more walls, I go and have a long sit in the student cafeteria.

Something there is very good—the food—and something else is very bad—a huge photographed wall mural of a deep green forest that makes me so homesick for Montgomery I want to cry. The incredible brunch bucks me up, though. I may be in the god-awful Women's College, but I'm still in Saudi Arabia, home of a lot of buddies over the years and great food. In the better mornings ahead this becomes my favorite daily meal—a brunch of eggs in a sauce, with feta cheese, olives, salad, *hubbs*, and tea. Salad with breakfast is a totally new and addicting idea.

I notice there are no teachers at all, even though heaping trays of fragrant food are nearly free, subsidized, and delicious. I'm thankful for the social break, pretend I'm in an Alabama forest, and start meditating on how much better life can be and how to change it.

In the blur of colleagues after breakfast, I keep my questions to myself, plan a double-date with the blond Texan and a weekend trip to ARAMCO with a very nice new teacher whose brother is a chemical engineer there. I find my own office and hole up in it as if in a cocoon. It's wonderfully quiet. Not a single complaining student shows up. I think they really have given up on me, and that part I don't mind, but what now? I'm afraid to move around. Every action I take seems to stir up trouble.

I can hear a lot of arguing down the hall and see senior instructors coming and going from the scene as if it's a football game requiring a lot more men off the bench. They all look unsettled, and the discussion level does not abate all morning. I have no idea what they're talking about and actually lack the emotional energy to find out, much less to take sides. When the Daraiyah crowd finally files out to their bus and hunches up inside, looking tired and spent from where I'm sitting, I begin to unwind and to wonder which *men* might supersede the *women* I'm dealing with here.

I write a short note to Dr. Budaire, head of all English study at both colleges, men's and women's, and submit it to intercampus mail:

> Dear Dr. Budaire—
> I am not happy at the Women's College. I seem inappropriate for the department specialization I may have poorly selected. Can anything be done?
> —Chris Cryer
> Foreign Language Department, Women's College.

An immediate reply the next morning puts my heart back on Easy Street:

> Christine Cryer—
> Do not teach any more. We are oversupplied with teachers this semester and you can be replaced in your specialty. You can substitute a few days this week in Sociology, then just come on regular hours to your office daily for the rest of the semester, and we will place you more effectively next semester. I'm sure you can assist with proctoring standardized exams and grading papers for some other instructors.
> —Dr. Budaire

Finding Our Way

Now that the Women's College is just a technicality, my creative juices are flowing. At great expense to the Saudis, who really don't care, neither Marc nor I have anything to do. I enjoy my brunches at school and do exactly as Dr. Budaire recommends, sit in my office from eight till one in case I might be needed in some auxiliary capacity. It would seem a fact that the Medical Department is glad I'm gone, and no one ever brings any papers for me to help grade. My Daraiyah associates are perfectly happy to see me at a potluck now and then and think of me more as an in-town social link than anything else. The hellacious sounds of discontent that I heard from senior offices continue much of every day but seem thankfully to have nothing to do with me, at least as long as I manage to remain unassigned and freewheeling in my office space.

I do sub in Sociology for a short time, and this too is amazingly detached from the rest of my career. I'm given specific Saudi history to teach from Saudi notes translated into English. So I'm now an instructor of Saudi history, something else I thankfully cannot possibly be expected to know anything about. And what an interesting occupation it is! I'm fascinated by the story of the rapid development of the House of Saud as tribal organizers and protectors of the wells. They have won over the hearts of the various nomadic factions by organizing the wilds into one communal territory. I find this tale of taming the land remarkably like the American signature history of pioneering and settling the West.

Mostly, I brunch and munch. The *collea* also hosts a daily tea time for girls, including a fully New Orleanian level of service and cuisine, demitasse tea with beautiful petits fours, different only in that the tiny cakes are not frosted on their tiny sides. Priceless as an experience, tea time is also cheap.

I love to watch the girls because their gowns (this is the only accurate description) and dressing are spectacular. I've worn such clothes only at balls and not many of those. Most of my Western friends have never owned dresses like these. In New Orleans in high school, my life, however, was somewhat ball-ridden. The students' long skirts are generally silk, and if not, then silky. Some, like ball gowns, are full-skirted and ruffled. Others are simpler and sleeker. It's a matter of personal style, but this is daily wear. No wonder drivers are situated outside to open car doors and glide these femmes fatales around town.

The tea room, which is slightly fancier than the cafeteria, collects all the heavy perfumes into a bouquet that is somehow acceptably harmonious. Earrings can be long, and most arms are golden almost to the elbow. Here's where the chattiness takes over, and the room is breathy with female excitement. It amazes me to see the difference in mood of the girls. They do take their classes seriously, much more than my American students, but throw it out the door at tea time.

I never ask my colleagues why they fear to trespass into tea and brunch arenas of the campus, which has, after all, little else and almost no books in English. I just go and watch, eat, and love it.

Well-fed and well-officed, I begin to see that my future comes down to my own initiative. I begin to plot ways to become a constructive citizen again. At home, Marc is in his heyday despite the lack of adolescent peers. He is someone I can learn from. He has not complained yet, though the central focus of the group of house-husbands he hangs out with is the worst of all subjects—housecleaning.

Potpourri of Worlds

Playing Hooky

SINCE I'M TOO POOR to send Marc to school and my skills seem too poor for me to teach, Marc and I essentially find ourselves alone in an underclass of moochers. We're somehow mooching off the Saudi state, and we no longer teach or learn; we coast. We're laughing at each other, but I'm not sure who'll get the last laugh. We won't feel the consequences of Marc's time-out for years, but there's something economically uneasy for both of us, as I sit in a vacant office, totally replaced and replaceable.

Part of every day, I replay Scarlett O'Hara's line in the face of shirked duty, "Tomorrow is another day." When I look up after saying it again, Marc is beaming. "I know you're not really tired from work or anything, but wait till you see the kitchen floor, and the bathroom, and these tools Robert and I got for doing floors." Not only is all my time free and most of my food subsidized, cooked, and served, but my apartment is sparkling! Minute by minute, nothing seems right.

In my mind I tell him to just stop this right now, that all this housecleaning is ridiculous. *What's wrong with him anyway?* Then I realize I don't mean that at all. Even though I don't mean it, the next line that goes with that trite, and for us inaccurate, conversation pops right up too. *Why don't you get a job?*

Just as I erase these inane, thankfully unshared, murmurings from my mind to wonder how he got the floors so shiny and where he picked up the great falafel he's handing me, he says it himself. "By the way, I got a job. Is that okay?"

"No, no, no! What mirror world are we in? I'm the one who's supposed to have a job, not you."

"You do have a job. But it's okay. Whatever you think. I was talking to a Saudi family at Diane's that has a real estate company, and all I'd do is serve tea. It's a full-time job though. They're a nice family, the Zimindars."

I don't really answer. I sit down and eat the falafel, look at the ceiling and the floor a lot, and feel even hungrier when I finish. I make funny eyes at him because he knows everything, and talking to him is sometimes less productive than just letting my histrionics fly. He actually deserves a huge hug, but that's the last thing he'd like, so I keep adding peace and space to a moment in our personal history that I will never forget. Your child before the first job and your child after the first job are two different people. I know this, and I know everything is happening too soon. So far, however, I haven't found another school for him.

"Marc, we might find a school for you. We should keep trying."

"Sure, but in the meantime I can make a mint, and as soon as you find a school, I'll retire."

"Well, I guess anything's better than cleaning too much. You didn't flood the tile floors with water and push it down those middle drains, did you?"

"Yeah!" he says. "That's how you do it. We got this giant squeegee and we're all using it on different days of the week. Look at this thing."

So I learn how to clean tile floors in Saudi Arabia and quite a bit more. I learn to step up my own campaign for normalcy in school and work before I'm found guilty of some infraction against Saudi child services. Diane, Larry, all their friends, not to mention the

Zimindars, however, assure me that, at least for now, Marc should serve tea. My other colleagues are less likely to understand.

I know now, many years later, that this is the hardest job of his lifetime. I also know that, like an athlete, he thrives on new disciplines. He's a young man not unlike biographer Henri Troyat's old Tolstoy in Moscow in the winter of 1882-83, who

> ...in order to "weave as little as possible" [morally] going down his road, got up in mid-winter while it was still dark, to the cry of the whistles summoning the workers to their nearby factories, did a few calisthenics with his dumbbells, dressed himself in peasant clothes, went down to the courtyard to draw the water, drag the huge tub through the snow on a little sled and fill the water pitchers; he split wood for the stoves, cleaned his room and then, sitting in the entryway, pulled open a drawer under a bench, took out wax and brushes and waxed his boots, proudly reminding himself that he had twelve servants and was taking care of himself.

Marc does not need the money either, but I think he does need this job.

Potpourri of People

There are stranger matters in our Riyadh life than the son working and the mother not. A certain ironic humor is weaving its way through every day. We live in a potpourri of worlds in which nothing is wrong exactly, but things seem sometimes somewhat backwards. I just checked the globe to note that we are close here to the exact opposite side of the hemisphere from which we came. This, of course, is graphic evidence of absolutely nothing, except that there are times when living here feels like that, as if no phone call from any phone center can ever remove the echoing that rings from the core of the earth to remind you that you truly have lost connection with what you thought you knew.

If such pondering seems preposterous, consider that the entire Muslim *Ummah* (community), spread across the complete world, prays five times a day toward the direction of Mecca. They are praying toward us according to precise Islamic physical calculations, all directed in specific imaginary lines, circling the earth like a ball of yarn. If these hundreds of millions of Muslims are sure that they project ideally from every point in the sphere to here, I am willing to consider my own lateral stupefaction. I feel eternally connected to Alabama by a long line stretching across the globe that has gone, unlike the Muslim prayer lines, askew in unexpected ways. Perhaps in Saudi Arabia one should get off old memory lines and onto a prayer rug.

Our power has gone out, not a common experience here, so Marc is advised by everyone on the penthouse floor to go to the power department for help. I'm suddenly glad and even a little bit proud that he's learned quite a lot of Arabic to speak. It won't be necessary at the power department but may help him to meet and greet. He also has, oddly, come to look like a Saudi, not just dress like one, but actually feel more comfortable dressed like one. He seems invigorated by the negotiation task, so I have hope of getting power back before dark.

I'm happy to have a break to sort out my thoughts in a quiet, power-less setting. I'm thinking about getting the power on, sending notes to various deans with new job ideas for myself, and sorting out my reactions to ARAMCO, where I visited last weekend. The ARAMCO trip made me realize that few Americans are doing what I'm doing in Riyadh. ARAMCO in Dhahran, a short flight away, is not like our potpourri of people, not an example of the 90-percent expatriates employed here, not the same melting pot of languages and lifestyles.

My colleague, who invited me to spend a weekend with her

brother's family at the oil company, is a dear kind of Dorothy from Kansas, who feels there's "no place like home." And amazingly, the ARAMCO compound is exactly like home. Once inside its walls, you feel you're in an American city, not a company complex with housing. As far as the eye can see are suburban-style streets and small houses with yards, running alongside parks where kids are playing baseball, no less. Their activity center rivals those in California's largest new development communities, and the people there wear shorts and Nikes, eat hot dogs, and watch the latest American films. They have everything we ever had at home, and seem to have no reason to go out into Dhahran.

We did go out of the compound to eat Saturday night dinner, though. My friend, her relatives, and I ate in a comfortable restaurant in the middle of a stingingly silent city. While ARAMCO is the state-owned national oil company of Saudi Arabia and the largest oil corporation in the world, it appears also to be the closest thing to home itself for its huge employee base. Americans were not strolling the streets in Saturday night fashion, nor were Saudis. There was no maddening construction, no hills bedecked with garish, lighted palaces reminiscent of Halloween celebrations at home, little shopping available, and none of those wondrous smells in the street that have caused me to ignore my own kitchen.

As I think about ARAMCO again, I realize that the KSU staff is largely isolated from the many Americans, Europeans, and other expatriates near us in Riyadh by virtue of their living and working in just such compounds, though all are far smaller than ARAMCO. Our employee guidebook wisely recommends buying a maximum of food items directly at the *souk,* the Saudi version of a farmers' market. But the three expats I know from Riyadh compounds have only each been once to the *souk.* Things are so convenient for them in their special worlds that they seem to stay there and live out near-perfect expatriate lives.

Like the Stepford Wives, these lives seem a little too perfect, too easy, and too separate. This degree of fantasizing about where you are can even be dangerous, as liquor is as illegal in Saudi Arabia as it was in the U.S. under Prohibition, despite one party I walked in upon from a major foreign communications company in which a lot of wonderful, sentimental singing was done on the part of a largely drunken crowd. I sat this one out on the company bus in the parking lot, with not much to read but napkin jokes and my grocery list.

Every week I have new perspectives on what it means to really be right here in the middle of Riyadh, so close to the famous Mecca I cannot visit, because it is a city for Muslims only, a sort of massive Vatican with no outside tourism. I hear now the *Adhan* for *Maghrib,* the early evening prayer, and think of the multi-millions of Muslims kneeling toward Saudi Arabia. They are more connected from Timbuktu than I am to any expatriate compound in the city. I go up to the roof to listen and watch the sun set, and I thankfully spot Marc coming up our street. It's gotten too dark in our supposedly powerless home to write notes to any deans. I have an idea our power is up and on and gesture to Marc in the street with questioning arms out to my sides like a priest at Benediction. He gives a thumbs-up and starts on up to the roof.

I wonder why I haven't come up here at sunset before. I watch the colors fade and hear the *Adhan* die out, setting another silent break. I check the growing darkness for the birth of tonight's first stars. They appear like the shining eyes of quiet children who want with all their hearts, from far across the world, to pray with Saudis here.

Marc has much to say and much he's learned. The power is on, but not because he filed a complaint. It's because the electric company clerks got to know him and felt they could not do enough for a young, slightly Arabic-speaking foreign head of household. They held their response till the end of an afternoon of sweet Saudi mint tea, drunk by full-sized men from tiny porcelain cups, under tents constructed outside for relaxing during the afternoon break.

Bedouins, Marc reports, are much the discussion in town. The Zimindars at the real estate office say builders are aghast to find that first-rate new and free public housing for them is both accepted and rejected. They're too often using the apartments received for TV and kitchen appliances only. The rest of the time no one has been able to convince them to leave their animals alone outside. The Bedouins prefer sleeping and relaxing with their tiny herds en masse in tents in the parking lot!

It seems the electric company clerks are nonplussed with the Bedouins for another reason. While they "religiously" follow intricate sets of rules of good conduct of a cultural nature, they're regularly skipping certain Wahhabi rules of religious life. Saudi locals apparently bounce between honoring their Bedouins and wishing they'd read their *Quran* more. This is a little like the modern American regarding the Native American sometimes as a noble savage and other times as just plain savage. Tolstoy strove himself to become like the Russian *muzhiks*, the people of the land, but it took him a lifetime of developing literary characters who strove the same to face the fact that neither his characters nor he himself would or could ever achieve the transformation from town person to ground person.

It is indeed a potpourri of worlds here, and I begin to realize the most important thing for Marc right now may not be enrolling in an educational institution. I see he's in a kind of school—the school of life.

The Palace and the Ivory Tower

An Audience with a Prince

I've decided we need help. Marc is acquiring a level of tea service taught in no culinary school in America. Tea is served everywhere here, in a complimentary way. Banks, electric companies, offices, even some shops serve tea to customers. He knows which cup is proper for what tea, what levels of boil and which leaves should be treated how. He knows the nuance of *Qahwa Arabia,* the exquisite thimble of tea-like coffee served fragrant and clear in tiny porcelains, and he knows *Turki* (Turkish coffee), and the regular mint tea served in narrow clear-glass demitasse. He preheats cups and teapots with introductory boiling water with the same flourish of the hand seen in Parisian crêperies, where the chefs toss their pancakes for flair and no good reason at all.

Al Zimindar has told me he thinks of Marc as a son. Marc says this is too true, since family relations, while tight and reliable, can be distinctly harsh. We need help to get this "scholar" back into school! Our Chinese Muslim friends who've lived their whole lives in Riyadh are the first to suggest a real solution. I play chess with them from time to time. Jian and I sit on the carpet, as most Saudis I know do, ignoring the fashionable Western furniture that seems mostly status symbol and not very sensible to them. We cogitate quietly more than any group I know, so I feel best asking her, her

husband, and her sister about schools and getting in. I'm not trying to make conversation. I'm asking the smartest local family I
know for real help.

Apparently, Marc, like me in my fantasies, is a sort of T.E. Lawrence. There are no other expatriates anyone can think of who ever
really want to go to a Muslim school. I do not understand how they
all afforded the American School, but I know I can't. It's clear that
long-term expatriates generally have no children, leave them at
home with relatives, or most amazingly, send their adolescents and
teens to Europe for school. Sending Marc away is the one thing I
would never do and find difficult to admire among my peers. If we
do not have the adventures of life with our children, do we have
them at all? Can the Saudi schools be so bad that no expatriate
would want to attend them, or is it that they are so good the Saudis
cannot possibly afford or desire to share them? No one seems to
know, so we accept the advice of Jian and her family. They will set
up an audience with a prince in Riyadh, who lives far from us, out
among the palaces. It is a solid Saudi tradition; anyone in Saudi
Arabia is welcome to bring problems to the nearest prince for advice and sometimes direct assistance. We go upon the proper day
and hour for an audience.

I have rarely been in these suburban hills lined with gargantuan homes and palaces, generally gated severely, often with armed
guards at the gates. The land itself seems rougher here than in
town, setting the homes and buildings high above the road on series of craggy and irregular lumps of ground with very little green.
The prince is not visited at his palace, but in a very mundane and
plain two-room office not far from the barren highlands we need
to wend our way through to find him.

The first room, a sort of waiting room, has simple chairs all
around its perimeter. It is dark and undecorated except for one
thing—an enormous picture in color of King Fahd. As I wait in a
full room of petitioners for a long time to see this prince, I have

a lot of time to think about the décor, the situation, and the very idea of taking a plea to a prince. I think the picture of the King an enormous irony, but one I've experienced many times before. Islamic tradition prohibits pictures of animate creatures. But the King takes exception to this in grand fashion! Even Mohammed is never portrayed in art; Islamic visual art remains confined largely to patterning of geometric shapes, celebratory calligraphy, and flower-design combinations still called arabesques.

The garish portrait of the King reminds me of a car trip three weeks ago with a male friend who has a car to Al Kharj to see an old fort about fifty kilometers from Riyadh in a valley where *wadis* (dry streambeds) meet. It is a wonderful structure to see, go through, and study, but we are stopped from taking pictures, in a somewhat frightening manner, by two guards. After that, I do not forget how seriously Saudis take the idea of people chronicling them on camera. My friend is an artist, so he sketches the magnificent but crumbling rampart and gives me his work. It seems invaluable because there is no other way to hold its image in our memories.

There is nothing animate about our sketch, but I have always noticed that Saudis in particular, of all my international students, love newness in buildings and décor. My Saudi students in Alabama had distaste for what we hold dear as antique. Since Al Kharj, I wonder if Saudis have a reticence to face warmly the meaner aspects of their past. Perhaps a shame of their old buildings and old cities explains the massive full-city renewal here that seems unthinkable elsewhere.

While personal (at home) picture sharing among Saudis seems the same as for all people everywhere, display of pictures of people is unheard of, especially publicly. Consequently, nothing can quite explain for me the Vegas-style treatment of the visage of King Fahd all over the Saudi world. He always, however, looks pleasant and on task. King Fahd, in all his benignity, gives me confidence at this moment, as the prince is gesturing for me to enter his small room, where I sit across from him alone at a large wood table.

Now that my time to see the prince has come, I am amazed by the simplicity. I am introduced by a second person, but feel all along that this meeting is between just the two of us and that all before me have felt the same. I should be nervous, but raised in what are now called convent schools for girls, followed by my Jesuit grad school, I have lived near-military intimidation all my life. This prince is a piece of cake, an earnest, relaxed listener, unhurried, and seemingly sincere.

This mild-mannered representative of King Fahd would never have passed initiation into the Jesuits, the guard dogs of the Church, who put the fear of God in me. He is imposing in no way and appears to be a man of few words. He wears nothing beyond the uniform of the elite Saudi man, a *thobe* so white it makes you squint, of silk and never simple cotton, with cuff links instead of buttons at the wrist. He does not wear expensive jewelry, probably because this is an Islamic convention of humility for men. Saudi men in general are not expected to wear gold or shorts either. The prince definitely maintains all the rules, is middle-aged, and seems kindly resigned to listening and responding in a calm and ritual way. You sense that he has done this for a long time and knows the questions to be asked as well as the answers that fit them.

The air of guarded protection that surrounds the palaces does not exist in this dear and dumpy double room, where I've already heard the woes of twelve people discussed in a language I can barely understand. Nothing seems secret or frightening, and the door between the two rooms remains open at all times.

"*Asalam alaikum.*"

"*Salam,*" he replies.

In the end, he promises to request that a boys' high school in downtown Riyadh, called Al Manarat, take Marc as soon as possible. We should wait for further information.

What is wonderful in this exchange is not just the encouraging answer to our need but the fact that a plea to a prince can work simply and quickly and be so direct and personal. There are no forms or files on hand. Nothing is written down by me or submitted, though the prince does, himself, take notes. There is no bureaucracy to go through, no secretaries or clerks to act as barriers. There are also no procedural directions available, written or oral. All of us lining the room seem to just know what to do and follow each other comfortably. I realize that seeing the prince is the same as asking for help from your congressman, a democratic institution to be thankful for, wherever I can find it.

In a matter of days Marc receives a tall stack of heavy textbooks in English, which look to us like gold. I think we both are likely to study them from stem to stern before he ever gets to class. An English textbook never looked so good. Based on these books, my impression of Al Manarat School is a good one.

Breaking Into the Ivory Tower

Marc's stories begin to feel predictable. He seems to be the strongest force in his own destiny, as once again, his establishment offerings are withdrawn while his street options skyrocket. Just as he starts to review his new texts, waiting for news of his forthcoming enrollment date, we receive notice that his option to enroll is being canceled. Some last-minute bureaucratic issue has arisen, and there will be no space for him after all. But true to his fortunes, he's simultaneously been offered office work in a translation company, and he is still only fourteen years old!

I am too weary to resist his choices and open doors any more. "Congratulations, Marc. What are you doing and what are you making now?" This is all I have the energy left to say. Among other things, I'm just a little jealous. "You're really street smart, but are you safe out there?" At this, he works up one of his demonstrative tea servings and replies with a story.

"Mom, you should not worry. Mohammed Zubi" (a twenty-five-year-old translator from Diane's group) "got me in, and I can ride with him." I know Mohammed and the other translators we know are in their twenties, work late, drive Mercedes convertibles to the juice cafes after work, etc., but they're educated men from good families. Amazingly, with no alcohol, bars, theaters, or dating, I'm less concerned for Marc to be out with Riyadh adults than with Montgomery adolescents.

"The thing that did happen," he begins his story, "was in the alley over there." He shows me the alley from the balcony window. "There are some kinda rad Saudi kids that spend a lot of time behind those trees over there, and they watch me. So I got stopped, and they were speaking Arabic and asking me questions, and I just didn't say anything, because I thought they'd notice something about my Arabic. They were trying to figure out who I am. After a lot of shoving and stuff, one just said, '*Entee Saudi*,' and they left. I guess they won't be interested in me anymore."

"*Entee Saudi*?" The resolution of this story is less clear to me.

"'You're a Saudi.' That's what they wanted to know, if I'm Saudi or not. They think I am. Ha!" What this means to me is that there is a tiny possibility Marc will have anything at all to offer the translation company. Maybe he'll help explain some English communications that come in from the U.S. "*Entee Saudi*?" This is a startling twist in an unplanned career tale.

Nobody loves picnics like the Saudis, and now that Marc is leaving the real estate office, his boss, Al Zimindar, has invited us both to an extended family picnic in the desert, where else? It's important to go now because winter starts soon, and the weather right now is as good as it'll be all year long. Zimindars will stay about ten days, but people bringing out supplies will come for a one-night overnight and I can come and go with them, while Marc can have a ten-day vacation before his new job.

This is another ironic Saudiesque reality. The people who have the roughest, least comfortable land in the world to picnic or camp on are the ones that identify with it the most. Picnicking and camping are definitely the national pastimes of Saudi Arabia, and I can hardly wait to go. But this is next weekend, and for now I am in a state of resolve to catch up with my son's career and find a way to have a one-on-one, heart-to-heart talk with my male boss, Dr. Budaire.

After some careful thought, culminating the last few months of lassitude at work, I determine to leave a message for my Women's College boss that I have gone to an appointment with Dr. Budaire and will not be in tomorrow. Rather than working a few more months at figuring out how to get such an appointment, I'll just find out the bus route to the Men's College, go there, and talk to him. I cannot explain what insane fog I am in, but the most obvious fact does not occur to me in my planning. The reason I do not know the location of the Men's College is that it's a *men's college* and no women are intended to present themselves. There is no reason theoretically for me to ever go there. But I am, and I do.

Budaire's Ivory Tower

Two busses and a short walk are supposed to land me in front of the Men's College. I don't want to say who told me, and I don't expect to even feel comfortable in that part of town. I've never seen the Men's College area, though I know I get the second bus near Bechtel Corporation, where I have seen memorable towers with armed guards, pacing *their* glistening walls. I'm sure my boss will think I'm meeting Dr. Budaire somewhere else, will assume from the note I left her that I would never go there.

In fact, Dr. Budaire does not expect me and may not be in, for all my efforts, but he's always been my Wizard of Oz before, and I need to find him. A stupid fantasy goes through my mind, in which I envision women outside the Men's College treated the same as men outside the Women's College. I see myself forcibly detained outside a guarded entrance, squatting in the dirt and smoking Beedis in the hot sun.

The second bus has only one other lady riding in our back section. When I reach to put some coins in the pay-box, she stops me: *"La! La!"* The women really do not believe we should pay, and there is rarely any money in the pay-boxes. She gestures for me to sit next to her, even though we are unlikely to talk. It takes two to hold up a pidgin English–pidgin Arabic conversation, and I'm usually the one to start, but today is different. I'm allowing myself to feel everything I've held back since the first week at the Women's College. I feel driven by another force, moving mindlessly toward the Men's College in a fitful reverie.

I am nothing here right now, not a teacher, and for the first time, not much of a mother either. The only thing worse than my current situation seems about to happen. It's almost winter, and I could easily find myself placed back into the next semester pool of teachers, in the eye of the storm I now am privileged to watch meekly from the side. I intended to be Chris among the Saudis, as I'd been many years with Saudi groups in Montgomery and Baton Rouge, and I don't appreciate the dog-eat-dog expatriate world speaking for me and defining my role. My colleagues are losing their jobs, dropping like flies, when I intended to work toward four years and a penthouse like Diane.

I numbly float off the second bus and down the road to an entrance to the college itself. I don't quite remember the trip I just took or exactly how to repeat it in reverse. Shocking in my state of malaise is the fact that the school is striking. It wakes me up to see it. It is not vaguely like the Women's College or any place I've been in Riyadh. It does not have a doorman, single floor buildings, thick adobe walls to hold out mud and dust from the street, weeds, or rolling thistles. Nor does this campus glow like the Blount project in Daraiyah. I see no marble, tiled terraces, fountains, tall buildings, arched corridors, or mosaics. It looks normal, Western, like our small liberal arts college in Montgomery. The Men's College is green, shady, pleasant, and for the moment open and quiet.

I'm taken aback. There's really no one this minute to see me enter. I can walk right through an opening in the airy fence that exposes grounds as far as I can see. My head is still numb, thinking of my Wizard of Oz. Is he there? Can I find him? Will he see me? No one I know has seen him since our interviews in Atlanta eight months ago. If he refuses to see me now, he will cast me back to the combined Wicked Witches of the East and the West. Like Dorothy, I want home, not to *go* home, but to *make* home and I cannot do it without this sage man.

My literary brain is frying with painful images I wish I could stop identifying with. It's bad enough to be afraid I will be stopped, but I'm feeling like Tolstoy's Anna K. on her way to throw herself under the train that brings her much-desired demise. She wants at her last promenade to kill herself; I only want to kill my worst of two personas, but a death is a death, and always a great moral risk.

Numb like me, Anna cannot chat with bystanders and sees the worst in everyone around her, as she convinces herself there is every reason to walk away from everything. Others, she thinks, see hope, but they do not know how hopeless life is. In the last flash of her consciousness, before the endless darkness underneath the train, she sees the most glorious memories, of laughter, joy, and connectedness. I share her dashed flash of past joy, but do not throw it out or myself. I hold it invisibly between my two hands like the magic dust that Peter Pan gets from Tinkerbell. I grasp it and I march in, smoothly, nonstop, checking myself, my skirts, my scarf, my eyes.

A young man passes me as if I am not there. I am incredibly thankful for that. When I see the second one, I calmly ask, with no eye contact, where Dr. Budaire's office is. Again, I am in luck. He points without stopping at the second floor of the building I'm approaching. *Sigh!* I imagine dispelling my gold dust in pure celebration, relax my hands to my sides, and enter the ivory tower at last, gliding like a ballerina, too quickly up the open stairwell to a broad floor of all open doors. Immediately, a man stands and exits his room to receive me, looking at me wordlessly with huge wide eyes. I say only, "Dr. Budaire," before he gestures and I walk in through the second open door to the desk of my Wizard himself.

I say it again, and he rises from his desk. "Chris Cryer…from the Women's College. I have an important question, and I thought I should come see you."

He is astonished, but polite. "How did you get here?"

"I took the bus," is my overly logical reply. I know he cannot think of what to say. He does not mean, "How did you get here?" He means, "How did you get *in* here?" But he listens to my incredibly quickly-stated case. "Since I have been extra in the teaching pool this semester, I want to suggest KSU consider my Childhood Education Master's in some way before the next semester is planned."

Dr. Budaire seems to see that the best way to deal with my intrusion is to answer my question directly. There is a good chance that my abrupt entrance can lead to an abrupt departure. "Yes, Rukaya Al Dayan at the faculty preschool in Daraiyah may be able to use you. I will have her call you. It is up to her entirely."

"Thank you, I'll wait to hear from her," I answer. I then smile and back out quickly, moving down the stairs and out the gate like a windswept ghost that doesn't want to be seen by anybody. I never hear mention of my "breaking into the ivory tower," and I never precisely confess to having made this trip to anyone. My bosses at the Women's College are already distanced enough not to care how my transfer has come about, but, *inshallah,* an immediate report goes out that I am badly needed by Rukaya Al Dayan, Director of the Faculty Preschool, for employment in Daraiyah. What I am to do there, rather like Marc's case, is yet to be determined.

As I bus home I have a chance to think about how my story can now change. I begin to calm myself and to lay my literary heroes to rest. Perhaps I have slain my weaker persona with some of the same kind of resolve that focused Anna K. Perhaps Dr. Budaire is my Wizard and the Men's College my Oz. Maybe now I will know my own powers and see how to make home where I am.

After Rukaya calls the next day and tells me how much she needs me, another book hero comes to mind, and he is one I do not lay to rest. I think with deep gratitude of what Antoine de Saint-Exupéry called determining true "matters of consequence." His Little Prince takes cosmic leave of his tiny asteroid planet in search of truth somewhere in the universe. After discarding relationships on various planets with annoying relatives, insensitive adults, and tight-minded bureaucrats, he learns from a fox in the Sahara desert how to live. By *taming* each other into a real connectedness, he finds he can finally have and keep heart. Even when the fox and Little Prince are not together, as tamed spirits they always have each other and real meaningfulness.

Thanks to my Wizard and Rukaya, my search is over, and like the Little Prince, I am revived.

Picnic Celebration

As if life were not glorious enough, it's time for the Zimindar picnic and campout. Marc and I spend a wonderful weekend out in the desert with a huge entourage of Zimindars and friends. They leave Riyadh in a caravan of several pick-up trucks full of supplies and several vans full of us. On the way, we are stopped by government representatives who try to discourage us from choosing the unpaved desert road we're on. Quite a brouhaha ensues, until finally we continue unscathed. The Zimindars are irate and claim this kind of prevention of use of lands they consider public is increasing, and not right.

I wonder, in such a young monarchy and loose conglomeration of tribes, how land distribution and use is defined. I know that young Saudi male adults each receive $100,000 or more to build or purchase property, and I know that Bedouins are offered free condos in Saudi cities. It is a wonder to see so much land, most of the country, uninhabited, open to picnickers and campers. In America and most countries I've ever visited almost all land is clearly privately owned, fenced, and closed to others. Here, we see no signs designating either parkland or private land. It's also different to live where almost all travel from city to city is by airplane. When we are out on one of the few major highways, we see few other vehicles, except for the many that have clearly been abandoned along the roadside as useless. They offer no restaurants, motels, or even gas stations.

That night we eat an extended *walimi* (feast) of barbeque, stuffed grape leaves, salads, cheeses, and warmed breads, preceded by hours of tea and followed by slow, small *qahwa* or coffees with pastries. We eat in the sand under the stars, cushioned by heavy, thick Oriental rugs. The exquisite Saudi *dullahs* (tall coffee pots with long, curved handles) sit atop makeshift grills afire. Tents are in the making and have been under construction all afternoon.

I leave Marc here for several days to celebrate his new job, as I am celebrating mine. Our host family is even more celebrative than we. They've just fought through seven months of disagreement about Zimindar's announcement to marry a second wife. Though plans were long under arrangement for a wedding to take place at this very time, the mass voice of family, friends, and associates has finally convinced him to cancel the wedding and go modern. I predict a happy future for all of us.

Lilliputian College

A Perfect Match

IF RUKAYA'D BEEN American, I'd have asked if she was a Kennedy. Tall, young, attractive, and self-assured in the face of her challenges, she has personally developed a Lilliputian college only yards away from the famed Blount campus-to-be. She serves faculty children three to five years old with a staff that has never studied child development in a country that has not yet opened childhood training programs. She stands calmly and confidently with one foot in the status quo and the other in modernization. We cross each other going opposite directions, and meet in the middle in a perfect match. She's moving cautiously toward the modernization for which I have a jaundiced eye, and I'm curiously looking backward toward recycling the best of the old. In the middle are wonderful kids who manage to disprove much of my Western training, making me wonder if culture can slip into the genes. Rukaya's little tribe is definitely *born* Saudi.

Dr. Budaire is like Rukaya. In Atlanta he seems like an Atlantan, but in Saudi Arabia he seems like a Saudi. When I break a primary rule, like hiking into the Men's College, instead of calling for the guards in an anti-Western huff, he gives me my Western minute and trusts me to gather my skirts and leave. These two are progressives in a country that needs them, able to play cultural hopscotch at a steady pace with no complaints.

They both give me my minute at the Lilliputian college. First, I am to look at everything in their medium-sized *elementary* school building and choose a spot for myself. I choose with some enthusiasm the kitchen, a huge set of related rooms not being used at all. The kitchen manager's office becomes my office, the kitchen center a classroom space for meeting with the preschool teachers, the kitchen phone the place to order my favorite old Daraiyah lunch from the Women's Restaurant.

Next, I am to observe needs and then suggest a job for myself based on those needs. The result is that Rukaya and I decide to set up child development classes in the kitchen and to send tapes of them to our dean, who is, oddly for us, in the Men's College Department of Geography. I try and somewhat succeed in imitating Rukaya's aplomb. I calmly cite a classroom of elementary-size desks in rows as an item for change, when Rukaya says it's not just the furniture that's too uptight, but the teacher for the same room. I am given the opportunity to reform this strictest teacher, who is otherwise slated for firing soon. It seems there are a lot of tears in her class and some of them are her very own.

What a wonderful cause for our classes! So, we begin, with lectures, discussion, materials making, and curriculum planning in the kitchen. It feels like a sewing bee. Everybody's ready for everything, though my target teacher with the straight rows is quiet.

On the playground I discover that the parallel play of three-year-olds in the West is totally absent. Each class plays as a cohesive whole, always picking a leader and following (yes, it's always) *him*. They also skip the exploratory sensorial play I'm used to in favor of a set game their little leader chooses. In all this there is just as much joy, grime, tumbling, and glee as ever. Maybe this early commitment to each other can help explain the Saudi social vision that seems to resist the fracturing of center we've come to tolerate in modern life.

All of our preschool teachers are young, educated Saudi or

otherwise Arab wives of faculty. They're bright enough and world-ly-wise, and like Riyadh women in general, rarely wear scarves in-side. When I tell them my training specialty is in the Montessori Method, a progressive Italian program, one teacher tells me her daughter attended Montessori school at Berkeley. Like Rukaya, these teachers live in a world of opening doors, and I get to open one more.

Somehow their building is wrong. It's for elementary school, not preschool; with materials similar to elementary materials, not sensorial or manipulative; the furniture too big and surely too structured for young children; huge, heavy metal and formica desks set in rows in rooms undeveloped for young movement and exploration. But the money for the program exists and the teachers know there is another more special treatment out there for young children. They simply have not defined it or designed it. You can always hear a pin drop when I lecture, then see a flurry of action. The teachers finish up class like high school seniors planning the prom. They know they'll get everything they want, and they want everything they can get.

One day, while cogitating what to do with the desks, texts, and almost insurmountable stairs our tiniest have to scale like moun-tain climbers at Everest, Rukaya interrupts my peaceful Women's Restaurant lunch. I'm lounging in my kitchen office chair, smelling and savoring selectively like a wine taster, when she comes. "Okay," she says, "let's really try it. Do you think you can open up one of these classrooms, set it up a little like Montessori, and teach with our teachers as assistants?"

"Sure. We can try, and we can see what happens."

"If they like it, then they can take back to their own rooms what they learn. You'll just have to go all around here and see what you can find to work with. I know it isn't much, but maybe there's enough for a short experiment."

"This'll be fun," I tell her. "I'll scrounge through all the closets and storage and see what I can find." I have that pre-Christmas feeling when you look for the presents you know your parents have hidden all around, in the attic, and under the beds.

Tolstoy and the Children

I think of Tolstoy at his beloved country estate, where he periodically gave up the frustrations of writing for the joys of teaching. He was torn between writing about the incorrigible sins of society upon peasants, while offering near-free publications for them, and just quitting writing altogether to create modern village schools. He was a bit sadly confused, not quite realizing for himself what a first-rate writer he was and what a second-rate educator. Anyone could have told him which was his true talent, but he vacillated.

Nothing thrilled him more than starting and reviving schools. Where there was dullness, he loved to stir the mind. Tolstoy, like me, thrived on bringing learning out of the most makeshift situations. He liked to teach where no one had taught before, something untaught before, to those who'd not been taught at all or not quite properly. His first classes were for his own laborers' children and neighbors in a large room on the third floor of his home. He was happy to write his own primary readers, publish them, train his own teachers, and spar with parents who expected corporal punishment. His situation of developing the school concept from heart, to mind, to some free space with begged, bought, and borrowed material was the same as that of Maria Montessori in early twentieth-century Italy.

They both rallied for what they called "spontaneous education." Tolstoy said it should "put compulsory schooling out of business." Troyat's biography of the great Russian describes what would have made Montessori and me totally at home:

The pupils came to the classroom as though it were home; they sat where they liked, on the floor, on the window-ledge,

on a chair or on the corner of a table, they listened or did
not listen to what the teacher was saying, drew near when
he said something that interested them, left the room when
work or play called them—but were silenced by their fellow
pupils at the slightest sound. Self-imposed discipline.

Maria's little charges became famous for blooming like intellectual
flowers at first in Italy, then in India, and now are often envied
across the world. My own preschoolers have always, amazingly,
done well too, but Tolstoy's were never seen as achievers. His were
the first Russian serfs emancipated in 1861 and even more challenged than Montessori's poor from the projects of Rome. I do not
in our case, though, expect to see anything stop our own privileged
and entitled faculty children, the "constrained" Wahhabis of Saudi
Arabia.

   As I rummage through the back rooms of Rukaya's white el-
ephant of a preschool, I do not feel alone. I know Tolstoy would
love it, and as for Montessori, I so sorely stuck out in my training classes as the sage and spokesperson of her philosophy, that
I wonder now if she speaks for me or I for her. My tiny kitchen
office and all the stuffy, dusty closets full of abandoned abacuses,
paints, chalks, and pictures of King Faisal are crowded for me with
the spirit of my mentors. They push me forward out of the office
and out of the closets, so that for the entire next semester I rarely
sit down again.

Taste of a Wedding Party

Rukaya also invites me to one of her sister's wedding parties. The
one I go to is not like a Western bridal shower, held by day in an
atmosphere of sunshine, pastel colors, pretty gifts, and frosting-
flowered cakes. It feels like a cool, trendy, underground nightclub,
albeit without alcohol or men. It's held at night in some rented
part of the Daraiyah complex that offers vast Casbah-style rooms

with arched doorways, polished cement floors, and ceilings so high that, in the darkness, you cannot find them at all. All the female neighbors, friends, colleagues, and relatives you expect at a wedding are also here at one of the week's many parties before the event.

The food is heavy, multiple fragrant dishes to help you last from five P.M. till ten or eleven, tables of salads and pastries, with servers on nonstop tours with trays of teas set in gold-rimmed cups with doilies. The atmosphere reminds me of fifties coffee houses my father escorted me to in my adolescence, before the tamed ones that reemerged in the current millennium. My father and I hung out near the art museums in Atlanta and New Orleans in dark basements offering classical music and cool jazz with German beer in brown and green glass bottles, husky smelling cheesecake that wasn't even sweet, and serious chess games not to be interrupted by a word of conversation, next to political hotheads who argued over each others' words.

Rukaya's party is the closest I've come to that sophistication I've missed. Set in dark and dramatic nightclub-style lighting, the discordant wailing of the female singer winds round and round the room hypnotically, deep thunder drums punctuating what sounds like painful ecstasy. Arab desert music has an ostinato beat that lulls you into its atmospheric plan, not sweetly like Bob Marley's, but temptingly like Carl Orff's set in the caves of debauched medieval monks. When the dancing begins, I almost ask the tea servers what the cover charge is.

There's no chess, but the conversation is multi-lingual, and the room filled with personalities, issues, stories, and more that I, in my limitation, am unlikely to interpret. Darker women wear richer, brighter colors, but no one wears pastels. There is such a thing as Islamic fashion, and it is here in deep winter shades of shimmering silk scarves, long, long earrings and the highest high-heeled shoes. Painted toes, ringed fingers, and gold-flanked wrists always dominate the Saudi woman's look, as a sort of last holdout for fashion extravagance, but tonight is so much more.

The dancing is as heavy and exotic as the dishes all around us. It's that mesmerizing sensuous seduction Westerners connect with the jeweled, perfumed, long-haired siren with the open midriff. When the bride-to-be enters, the ladies stand, clap in rhythms that get loud and louder, and finally exult in the grand and famous high-pitched Saudi yell of celebration. These dances, once started, continue all night, and we are all expected to take turns. This is very hard for me, and I do not even try. Sadly, I was no better in high school than now at lowering my inhibitions.

The political conversations rival those my father raised me on in the beatnik cafes. There is an endemic political mindedness in the Arab world that seizes both men and women. Our wedding party pushes on past ten and is in no way immune to issues of government or the sharing of partisan opinion. Such discussions run deeper in the late hours.

Never a party person, I am the first to leave. On the way home I remember a visit to a beauty salon with one of my former sociology students the week before her wedding. She wanted me to see all the preparations made for the honeymoon. Americans will one day embrace tattoos, piercing, even henna colorings for palms and finger tips, but none of this seems attractive or comfortable to me in the 1980s. Taking off all hair that can possibly detract from beauty, including everything below the chin, seems a slow and painful process. But this warm wax treatment is accepted, I know, with the same forbearance Americans lend to half-day hair treatments that move in rounds of chemical and electronic tortures. I guess I'd make the kind of fiancée who'd be happiest eloping.

What captures my attention and stays in my memory is less the beauty treatments than the salon itself, especially since it's walking distance from my apartment. I don't think about it much while I'm there, but afterwards I realize that I do not see another public commercial beauty salon anywhere in Riyadh. Of further note is the fact that the one I visited is a converted apartment, does not have a sign, and is located in a particularly clandestine corner of its building.

In Sherlock Holmesian tradition, I begin to realize that all of the beauticians appear to be Filipina. "Aha, my dear Watson, I wonder if there is some connection and story in this matter." These observations fit interestingly with recent local news, in which a Filipino has been found guilty of rape, causing the Saudi government to declare a cease-and-desist order upon all Filipino work visas with the mandate that Filipinos return to their country en masse. Exceptions, of course, are made for Muslim Filipinos.

There is much talk in Riyadh about this situation, and just as the few criminal cases that surface are dealt with remarkably quickly, so the Filipino population immediately responds by becoming Muslim overnight in astounding numbers. At any rate, I am able to conclude that neither beauty salons nor Filipinos seem much favored in Riyadh. I feel forced to cancel my plan for that first salon haircut away from home that I want so badly. I'm not ready to take sides on either Filipinos or salons.

Ups and Downs

Winter

WHILE THE PRESCHOOL blooms, winter comes, and it takes full hold of Riyadh. This sounds like an anomaly not to happen in the Great Arabian Desert, but it does, and with a vengeance. The city becomes uncomfortably cold every day, and most amazingly, it rains, which would seem a cause for celebration. In fact, rain in Riyadh proves an unbridled threat. In the expatriate world no one has raincoats, boots, umbrellas, or any idea what to do with what rain means, and we're shocked to find it means public disaster.

Certain neighborhoods close down after each flash flood, and they're erratic and frequent. Saudi desert rains hit more suddenly with greater-than-average downfall and drop on hard ground that's less prepared to absorb water. As a result, cholera surfaces, after we've all already seen some colleagues succumb to hepatitis in the fall. Public service announcements keep the disease topic on our minds, and cholera now tops "teacher firings of the week" for table discussion.

I stay out of cordoned-off areas and generally out of the rain, but one male friend with hepatitis worries me, so I visit him. Visiting is exactly what we're told not to do, but that's why I feel I must. He can only be lonely and depressed. I'm surprised he hasn't returned to London permanently, as he's quarantined the entire second semester. On the bus, on the streets, and in his apartment hall, it's cold. No one ever suggested I bring warm clothes to the desert, and now every day I'm freezing.

On my way to see Joel, I pass plenty of places to buy sweaters and coats, but the prices are exorbitant. In Riyadh there is nothing but the best, and at that a rush of demand. I dream of the coats in the windows, mostly from Paris, all at $600 prices that are over my head. The shoes and other leather goods are generally from Italy, and the jewelry true gold from the gold *souk* that sells by the daily price per ounce. There's not much hope for me and my budget. Even if I borrow from Marc, we're both too cheap to pay these prices. On the way to Joel's, I spot a delicatessen, where I can look for a gift for him.

I get almost everything in these little cellars of goodies—eggs, milk, soups, soap—and save for the bakeries the buying of fresh hot *hubbs*. Most of these goods are subsidized and always cheap. But this time, the minute I step down into the beds of sweet-smelling fruit tables and pass the spice shelves, I see something different, a wonderful, hideous pile of something that looks warm, hunched up like refuse in a back corner. "Oh, *inshallah*, that's not a coat, is it?"

"*La.* That's just Bedouin clothes. For men."

"*Inshallah. Inshallah.* Let me see." When I see what it is, my frozen, depressed winter spirit softens. "*Mush mushkillah.*" (No problem.) "I have never seen anything better!" Three thick woolen coverings with sheepskin lining, no buttons, zippers, or any closings at all, with long droopy sleeves like a king's robe, gray in color, all decorated Saudiesque in thick black ribbing in curls and swirls around the edges and along the openings in the front. I hold one up and it has the shape of a silk Mandarin coat, four feet across in a huge shapeless block.

"I love it. *Kam fulus?*" (How much?)

"You don't want that. It's just for Bedouins to wear on camels. It's only eighty riyals." (Thirty dollars.)

I leave in this wonderful coat that looks and feels like a blanket, but still has a curiously lovely line to it. In my imagination, my Bedouin coat can be seen as high fashion on the world's most famous models, making its way along the runways of Paris, receiving the same *oohs* and *ahs* from others that it does forever from me. So, I visit poor Joel in fashion and warmth, bringing him fresh fruit from the Mediterranean, and a few days later hawk the other two coats to colleagues from the Women's College to endless *ooh*-ing and *ah*-ing. I'm not the only one who's cold.

I'm happy to see Joel's stamina under duress. I am the only one to visit him this month, but he's a man of letters, and his interests are sustaining him. The quiet in his apartment, though, is a spooky, unfamiliar sound for me. As I leave the narrow halls of his building and listen to his elevator creak as I go down, everything there seems fraying, vulnerable, and at least for the moment, abandoned.

In our second month living in Daraiyah, I had a few days of flu and was sicker than I realized. Marc feared the worst for me one night at two A.M. and went to a physician neighbor for help. This was all unknown to me in my pain, until I looked up from my bed to see the gentle doctor and his wife together, bending over me with liquids and aspirin. I thought how kind it was of everyone to care, Marc, the doctor, and his wife, a good Muslim lady who would accompany her husband to a woman's bed. That night I told myself to visit the sick.

Saudi Arabia has nationalized health care, delivered for us through the university system. I have my annual exams with a female gynecologist who is quite the same for me as at home.

Watched, Taped, Chased, and Suspect

The best coat in the world cannot warm all the harshness of winter. Other things are chilling my spirit, as well. Creating a new job for yourself can be expected to have its complications, but I don't anticipate problems collecting my paycheck each of the next two months. I immediately report this glitch, only to be asked to be patient while the system adjusts to the fact that, while I am supposed to get paid at the Women's College two miles from home, I am no longer working there. I make several heartbreaking foot trips to the payroll office, where lady clerks seem as confused about my case as I am. Also, my happy home has grown silent. Marc now has an exactly opposite schedule to mine, so that he comes in when I'm sleeping at night, and I leave in the morning while he's still in bed.

Before this silent era sets in for us, I grew tipsy with the new spirit of the house, Marc bringing in not just Fahd, his neighborhood Saudi teen friend, and Narayan, his American friend, son of an instructor from Louisiana, but increasingly the young adult translators he works with, who are graduates from Turkey, Palestine, and other places. I was taken aback by the sound of so much Arabic in the house, and felt this intelligent nuance a grand surprise and achievement. I knew Marc could not read or write Arabic, but I played games with myself from back rooms to see if I could isolate his voice from others' in Arabic conversation. Often, I was wrong.

Now that I'm alone, I think too much. I'm not worrying about Marc, as before, but things I used to overlook with humor now mount ominously, creating an air of a gray, cold winter filled with only one good thing now, Lilliputia. I'm wondering why I have to turn in a tape of each training lecture given to my preschool teachers, though. I'm wondering also why at least once a week our building manager follows me when I'm shopping. I'm wondering about some serious encounters with moral police too.

While my empty bank account, empty nest, and "Big Brother"

atmosphere are weighing in, I decide one day to try again for the paycheck. After a full day of work and my now usual taxi ride home from Daraiyah, I leave my briefcase in the apartment and set out on the walk to the *collea* payroll office again. I prefer the exercise to the bus, and I like the homey, tree-lined streets. I actually want to get out into the world and see more people. Our house seems like a mere memory of last semester, with nothing to offer anymore. It has more smells than sounds. I smell the ground cardamom from Marc's tea prep and the laundry soap when I walk past the washer. These smells seem more alive than I feel. I want to go out.

Forty minutes later on the same track, shuffling back, I'm empty-handed and wondering as I did last semester if we didn't really come here for Marc to work and not me. I am working, and I love it, but it doesn't seem right that he's the only one with money. Today the walls around all the houses close me out, and my coat is warm but my hands are cold. I feel homesick.

Everything that's different feels wrong, unfair, and unkind. I'm sure I'm the only teacher in the system whose lectures are taped. We've been laughing about being followed by Abu Budi, our building manager, when we're out, and we always just turn around to him and say, "*Asalam*," but today, if I see him, I will surely lose my cool. The *matawas*, the public moral street cops, are out there too, much the topic in our group, and today, not such a joke to contemplate as before.

While I shuffle sadly, I start to cry and discover that I need to. I stop to consider that every person who has left their country for another for a long period must have felt the same, at least once. I'm sure they've all cried, and I am determined to express my equal rights as a displaced person. I cry wetly, too wetly for five o'clock in winter, even for Riyadh, which after all was supposed to be warm, not cold and wet! I tuck my hands inside my wide-armed camel rider's robe and rub my tears off, using it like a towel roll.

I thought I had a family. I thought I had a paying job. I don't think I am a criminal requiring surveillance, and I wish the international phone center could be used under the fifty-dollar minimum without such a stinging echo that you can't hear anyone on the other end.

As I shuffle along sobbing, a young Saudi boy my son's age comes up to me. *"Collea?"* he asks.

"Yes. I'm coming from the *collea. Abla.*" (Teacher.)

"British?"

"No, American." I feel he's very sweet and trying to distract me from crying.

"Okay?" I don't quite answer. "You cry."

"Salam. I'm okay. I'm sorry. I'm fine. I'm just a little homesick." I'm not sure he understands *homesick*.

"Where your home is?"

"Oh, the South of the U.S. I'm so sorry. I'm really okay. It's just a bad week and my money is late. *Mafi fulus ilyaum.*" (No money today.) *"Mush mushkillah."* (It's okay.)

"Maswat hene, tayib?" (I'll walk you home, all right?)

"Oh no, I'm fine," I say, starting to pay attention to the conversation and to forget myself.

"You sad of your country?" It's clear this young man intends to walk me all the way home, so we chat about Riyadh and Montgomery, and my cheeks dry. He climbs all the way up the stairs to our apartment, and as we pass Abu Budi, so curious at the front door, I feel better escorted than ever, and give Budi my severest nod. The young man waits till my huge and heavy door is unlocked and open, says good night, and leaves. Down the hall, he shouts back at me a final question, "You're good in Riyadh?"

"Aiyawa—Shokran. Ma Salama." (Yes—Thank you. Bye.)

This dear street guide is an angel. He brings me back to why I love the Kingdom and to the healthy recognition that we—okay, I—may be creating at least some of my own misery.

But, while Marc is not around to advise, escort, or make fun of me, things keep happening that sit in my soul like lead. Diane and some other ladies come down to get me on a Friday afternoon, which is the weekend in Riyadh, and after three near beers each, feel just as drunk as on real ones, and we all go off to the *souk* to "make the scene." Better we should have thought of it in other terms. While looking at bright and flouncy clothes apparently deemed tasteless by Wahhabis, we find ourselves in the midst of a *matawa* "attack."

Without sirens or flashing lights, these cruel male seniors, who are full-fledged, though possibly volunteer, police officers, raid the stalls. Their raid is exactly the same as being caught drinking in an underground nightclub in the U.S. during Prohibition. We all scream in concert with the local women, and everybody runs in scattered directions that best suit their escape. Some hide in the fold of the curtains behind the tables; others jump into vehicles, rev, and run. Our group, fortunately, goes pretty much the same direction but into a frighteningly open space, nonetheless behind the focus of the *matawas* who are yelling at shopping women and striking wildly with sticks. One friend is struck, but she says later that it didn't hurt through all her winter clothes, her long skirts and *abaya*.

We hide out in the nearest restaurant in a family eating section and tell our stories. This is nobody's first bad moment. It's hard to understand *matawa* law. What rule were we breaking? Do they know we had pretend beers? Can that be illegal? Is it the flouncy clothes we like that offend them? Should we be escorted at all times on the street? None of these things seem by *Quran* or by popular culture to be unacceptable. I tell my story about being chased out of Al Kharj for taking pictures of a building that's of international tourist interest. Then I let down my guard and tell what I've not told before, not even to Marc.

The day of the Al Kharj trip with another teacher, a male one, we stopped at a gas station on the way back. As we began to park, we noticed a police vehicle and started to think better of stopping. But, as if the police sensed our discomfort, they got out of their van and came directly to us. They asked us, though calmly and politely, not at all like the infamous *matawas,* to show our IDs. Then they asked if we were related. This was the leaden issue that scared me totally. We were not related, and we had heard that it can be a serious matter for a woman to be out with a man she is not related to, but it was such a matter of course in Riyadh so far for both of us that we never anticipated this moment of "truth or dare."

We also had no opportunity to consult each other in order to plan a consistent response. I thought of all the cop films I'd watched in my life in which they separate the suspects to check one story against the other. We had to answer on the instant, and the question was addressed to me. In the most morally disingenuous moment of my life, I calmly said, "Yes, we are." My friend said nothing, but held his poker face well, and warmed my heart with his support. It was a great opportunity for him to cut and run on *my* offense. He could have claimed anything that would sound manly and gentlemanly to the Saudis and been exempt. It was my own duty to protect my honor here, which translated for me, in those pressured ten seconds of hysterical consideration, to my own duty to lie for that honor.

The officers were in a position to insist on proof of how we were related, or so it seemed to me in my disempowered state. Instead they just asked more. How were we related? Hoping we would not both speak up at once with different answers, I said my friend was my cousin. The officers looked at papers for several minutes more, asked what we were doing that day, and let us go. To this day, I cannot psych out what the other ending to this story could have been, and after much restaurant talk and a lot of tea and dessert, no one comes up with a conclusive answer to how bad a story that could have become.

On the way back, my lady lunchers and I, already feeling like outlaws of the state, find ourselves compelled to commit greater atrocities. We know the alleged location of an underground Catholic church, so we hang out till mass time and go there, sleuthing like undercover agents. The building is a good one, suitable for overt or hidden activity, but has no sign, and surely no one standing around in black cassocks or fingering rosary beads. (Oddly, Muslims have similar beads for meditating.) Inside, everything is normal to the universal Catholic mass as I know it and knew it growing up in an Irish Catholic family.

Since I'm already in a bad mood, though, coming here only makes it worse. This is exactly where I always went in the States to try to lift a mood, and it has never worked. Just as in the U.S., I come and go, repeating the rituals of my distinct cultural lifetime, without a single person giving eye contact, greeting me in any way, or in particular needing my input or sharing theirs. My father always timed the sermon and recounted any minutes over fifteen, each of which he considered a criminal intrusion on our beautiful Sunday outing. We generally followed mass with a pancake breakfast, the part I still love.

Consequently, the winter does not drag on in bleakness and coldness after all. It leaps forward in harsh ways that keep me on my feet. The idea of being escorted, that I embraced with joy and fun when we first moved into our Riyadh apartment, is now gone by circumstance, and I miss it. Life is cozier and kinder with your escort on site.

The Up Part

My paychecks finally arrive, however, and the prospect of being better recognized in my new job code by the payroll clerks is reassuring. The phone rings and Rukaya says to come in early because there's hot news from our geography dean about all my lecture tapes they've been listening to. They have a new plan, and it's a good one. Rukaya and I have to meet first. Then I'm to meet with the dean.

The next day, I rush out earlier to grab a cab on the busy corner of our block, and get in rather distractedly, paying more attention to my notes, my scarves, and my curiosity about my opportunities than to the taxi driver. The day Dr. Budaire gave me permission at the Men's College to go to Daraiyah to work, he asked me how I'd get there daily from downtown Riyadh, more than thirty minutes away. I told him I'd work it out myself, and he seemed satisfied with that.

That means taxis every workday at quite a cost, but I decide it's worth it, though most female colleagues have never taken a taxi because they don't trust the drivers. Expatriates always tell stories about women kidnapped and hauled off into the desert. In fact, this is a familiar fear my family has had for me about the Arab world in general.

I tell the driver that I want to go to Daraiyah, a route I know so well I could map it in the dark. But he does not answer me, which is, after all, the duty of a taxi driver, and he seems more distracted than I am, which is too distracted. Immediately, he turns the wrong way and drives too fast in the exact opposite direction. "*La!*" I yell. "*Mafi Daraiyah.*" (This is not toward Daraiyah.) Instead of replying, looking at me, or turning around, he pushes forward in the wrong direction, singing weirdly the whole time.

Worst case scenarios take immediate hold on my imagination and throw me into an emergency mode. With difficult students and children, I always try to understand them first, and try to get on their side, so I pause a moment to consider this driver may just be confused and thrilled with singing. I watch his movements, reactions, driving, and listen to his mindless melody just long enough to decide he's not a confused singer. He's insane. He's doing everything badly, unsafely, and cannot be communicated with.

Quickly, he reaches the far side of downtown, the opposite of the Daraiyah side, the wrong side, and begins to slow because of heavy traffic. As he approaches a traffic light in an eight-lane highway strip, I see that there is nothing beyond the light but empty desert. There is no way this is my request or destination under any circumstance. So, I yell at him again, hoping to get him to stop at this last commercial corner and light. "*Halas! Hene!*" (Stop! Here!) I yell it twice, give up, open my door, and throw myself out of his slowing but moving vehicle into middle lanes of the giant highway and somehow come out standing straight and able to make it to the curb.

I don't like to tell this story in case my family and colleagues are right and I am wrong in such life choices, but life goes on, and this is meant to be a great day for me. So I cross the heavy intersection under the next green light and go to a food shop where they call me another taxi. I get in the second one, turn around, and arrive in Daraiyah late, but not too late to attend the most important meeting I've attended yet. Our geography dean, Dr. Alfani, wants to start the first college child development department in Saudi Arabia, and he wants me to write the proposal and form a task force to design it.

The U.N. and High Tea _____

The World of Assent

T HE RAINS STOP, and the sun is back, putting color into life again. Marc cuts his hours just enough for bedtime tea chats, and he's now brewing chamomile. I'm so glad to see him, I feel like he's back from the wars. I lose my grounding in Daraiyah, though, and can rarely return on the new schedule Dr. Alfani has set. I pay off and close my account with the Women's Restaurant and move into an office-less round of high-level administrative teas. Fortunately, the players are special, front runners in the Kingdom in child development, and there's a sense of celebration of what I call Rukaya's Lilliputian college.

Tolstoy never imagined so much assent, and Montessori rarely knew it herself. His desire to bring literacy to the masses was regarded more than suspiciously by his government, causing police raids on his home, classes, and records. Montessori pioneered more painfully than most Saudi women. As the first female physician in Italy, the single lady intern in her medical class, she was banished to dissect cadavers alone at night in the basement of her school.

But modern Saudi government knows the importance of universal education and begins to see what few do yet, the power of loading it into what Montessori called sensitive periods of development, most of which fall long before public school usually begins. The Saudis also see that women's education is significant, with their long-established mirror universe for women: women's banks, women's schools, women's clinics, always "manned" by female professionals.

My Daraiyah lecture tapes have been reviewed to raves and are set aside for future use. And I thought that, like Tolstoy, I might be guilty of breaking some government standard, that my classes, like his, would soon be raided and condemned. My teacher-students and Rukaya are now running our "open classroom" themselves. We save the endangered teacher who was about to be fired. After several weeks in our pilot "children's house," she is more relaxed than her children, and is the first to push her steel desks aside for more movement and creative work. She understands now that structuring and child discovery can be in contradiction. Her group now hums like a little village, caring for little friends, pets, plants, and their mini-kitchen.

Circle time for kids, sitting on the floor together for singing, hand play, stories, and presentation of phonics and numbers is an immediate success, as Saudis are ever floor people, who surely felt pressured into their former symbolically educational desks. While we lack the famous Montessori didactic apparatus, hands-on manipulatives to teach basic skills and subjects and we lack the training to use them, our group is still refreshed. Now they have open classrooms for free interaction and choices of materials from shelves arranged by subject and difficulty. It feels like an inviting home full of children now and not like school!

Dr. Alfani
I am asked to write the initial proposal for KSU's first preschool education program, but this story seems less mine than Dr. Alfani's. How he feels in charge of programs that are always attended and run by women I do not know. But he is a patient, comfortable,

grandfatherly man, who cares enough to do it in a way that will work and that can keep us all comfortable together. In Daraiyah, I never see any fathers at the preschool, though the children are little girls *and* boys. Alfani now sets meetings for us that generally include other women and me, and he is almost always the only male. Yet, he regularly arranges private transport for me now with a kind eye, as if he knows the difficulties for women moving around Riyadh alone. In fact, this is surely not a lifestyle he understands first-hand. But he picks up on my specialty immediately, and when the Montessori materials catalogue arrives from India with pages of text in Arabic on see-through parchment imposed between pages, he's as delighted as I am.

He announces between cups of tea in our comfy conference room, attended by another American preschool director from Riyadh and me, that we have received U.N. funding for our project and will travel together to look at some of the best Saudi preschools to date. I know this is awkward for him, so I'm happy when he adds a school he likes a lot himself, a military program for four hundred four- and five-year-old boys! The very idea is a curiosity, so many young children in one program and military school at such an age? But tit for tat, one for him and one for me. The Dhahran school reputedly has boys and girls together and is remarkably progressive. I wonder, after my own training, what that means to Saudis.

Alfani's military preschool proves to be a man's world, a little man's world, in a monolithic structure of buildings surrounding a parade ground of pure hard Saudi dirt. It's the closest thing to a castle with jousting court I've seen in Saudi Arabia. At first it seems unimaginable, like a Nazi plot to control the youngest male minds. Then, I see the Saudis have more in common with the Chinese on this project, as hundreds of bubbly little boys pour out of surrounding halls onto the parade grounds with high-pitched squeals of excitement, each group with its own cloud of different-colored flags, and snap together upon an instant in response to a single sharp whistle call.

These little guys perform for us with all the energy of a Mickey Mouse four-hundred-man salute at Disneyland. I've never seen so many little people so happy at the same time in all my life. Their marching is manly and stern and their flag work pure ballet. Before this demonstration, I sincerely did believe that only the Chinese trained youth this well for mass performance.

We move on to see their facilities, which prove the perfect balance, though probably expensively constructed—two dozen one-floor cottage-like little buildings, all with doors open to the sunny day. Each cottage is a classroom for no more than twenty boys, and across from their shaded walkways are medical rooms for dental and general health check-ups and gym rooms. This national health care project seems a perfect idea. Why not deliver care *at* school? I cannot stop myself from holding this idea exultantly, as if any government anywhere is likely to ask my opinion. Their little cottages are filled with maps, globes, chalk boards, and encyclopedias. In its own way, this school is as homey as our coed plan in Daraiyah.

In future meetings, I'm unable to say a single thing against the military preschool. Apparently, their test results are amazing, not to mention their health statistics. It never before occurred to me to consider how much some, boys especially, at certain ages may be turned on to the physical challenge and discipline of the military.

Three of us fly to Dhahran together and are picked up by Sally Turki and driver. She's a thirtyish American educator married to a handsome Saudi named Khalid. The school she shows us is clearly the only one that can possibly rival the military preschool. When we pull up to the school building, I'm sure we're at an intermediate stop. This, I decide, is an international bank building, not a school. It's important to remember that Saudis are a little ashamed of their poorer buildings and extraordinarily satisfied by their spectacular ones. Someone deemed that this preschool warrants the respect given the Taj Mahal.

We enter an open-floor building rather like Grand Central Station in Manhattan. A spiraling staircase off the marbled front hall swirls in stately manner up to the skylight ceiling almost thirty feet above. Ahead is a huge room of polished white marble floors, reminiscent of a main concourse, and it's lighted by rows of twinkling chandeliers. Still, there is no sign of a school, much less a down-sized one to house life's tiniest people. It occurs to me that preschoolers here might be on their best behavior, thinking they've died and gone to heaven, where such things are expected. Reflecting on Daraiyah, I recall how inhibiting our elementary desks were for preschoolers. Someone here does not know that children in wide open spaces universally feel a call to run, jump, and probably scream for fun.

But Sally is comfortable here and comes in behind us. "The classes," she says, "are all off this room." Only then do we notice an entire subculture of small beings milling around in smaller rooms all along the sides. It seems that someone, after all, in this land of plenty and wide-open space, did know to create small classes for small groups so young they call anyone *Baba*. (Daddy.) Immediately, I realize. Oh, my God, these are all Montessori classes! All of them! For months, I've been working to describe and explain Montessori methods to Alfani and the other ladies, who mostly nod politely, and now here we are in the biggest and shiniest Montessori preschool I've ever seen, heard of, or even imagined.

I try to count the classrooms but lose count. We're allowed anyway to spend as much time as we like and to visit in and out of the rooms that really are, as Montessori coined them, each a *children's house*. Some children are chatting in reading corners, others sweeping up table crumbs with the famous crumber tool, others engaged with a teacher in math computation with counters and beads. I am as completely at home as if I were in Cincinnati where I trained under one of Montessori's own first teachers.

However, I notice Alfani is not with us. Retracing my steps, I see he is still at the front door, negotiating entrance. He's in the mirror world, the women's world, now, and suffering everything a woman does at the military preschool. I know it's partly from moments like this, when he is himself on the outside, that he gains his skill to be such a gentle gentleman. I go out to try to help him negotiate, and Sally comes rushing right behind. "It will just be a few more minutes, Dr. Alfani. I want all the classes to know to expect you. If you don't mind? Oh, I can bring you some water while you're waiting."

I would not make a good Saudi of either gender, as I am unable to continue my tour for watching Dr. Alfani receive and drink his water and wait for permission to join us. It's imaginable that he hates this job, one in a department of all women, but I think not. Once again, he is an angel, and I—in fact all of us—really need him. It seems many men are suited to the angel task.

"Dr. Alfani, you can't imagine it, but this is a Montessori school! Huge, but a Montessori school. Why didn't they tell you? You didn't know, did you?" The site is absolutely breathtaking, a Saudi version of a grand Italian learning experiment. Alfani has almost nothing to say, though his countenance is on hold in his benign mode. He is ready to see it and begin to understand. The point for me, of course, is that now there is little doubt my request for this method will win.

Dhahran in the Vanguard

Between our tour and dinner, Sally Turki stops at her home to pick up a few things. She has no idea how fascinating it is for me to be for a few minutes in her milieu. She is the only American woman I know or am ever likely to know to marry a Saudi. After a lifetime of press stereotyping Saudi men as sheiks who live in tents with large harems of abducted women who are made to dance seductively on call, who would not be curious? Sally and Khalid are, contrary to stories, both young, bright, modern, and well-suited to each other.

They disprove the ghastly stereotype of the famous American silent film, *The Sheik*, starring Rudolph Valentino. It features a British debutante, abducted by Ahmed Ben Hassan in the dead of night into a guarded erotic harem in the blistering Sahara. Fortunately, sensitive viewers even then believed in Sallys and Khalids, as writers and directors depict Diana falling in love with Ahmed on first sight. She completely breaks with her boring British suitors to pursue the desert and hang around Ahmed's encampment, where her enemy proves to be, actually, the hero, who waits patiently for the divine first kiss that proves true love can always be pure and sweet.

Our contemporary sheik, Khalid, enters the living room briefly to greet us and to explain his own hectic multi-tasking. Like two busy American spouses, he and Sally ask each other questions from adjacent rooms, answer them short form, close on a loving comment, and pass each other in the hall with only a half-glance. But the Turkis each make time for me, even when they lack time for each other. They check cross messages on the same important local projects, point out souvenirs of their education projects, and usher us back to Sally's driver. Even their apartment I remember over time because of its handsome, stark modern quality with lots of white, straight lines and light wood. Their whole world seems in the vanguard compared to Riyadh.

Hospitality is a famous Saudi virtue, but I detect more here. I detect two highly intelligent people, committed to each other, the same tasks, and to us, the colleagues. They're somewhat famous in Dhahran, and not for their international marriage. They have that special charisma of movie stars that makes you wish you were them. I imagine what it would be like if I responded to an offer from one of the Saudi families that keeps urging my introduction to their brother, cousin, or uncle. There is only one Sally and Khalid, but today I sense that my reticence may well be my loss.

At dinner the vanguard testiness of Dhahran plays out what must be a nightmare for Dr. Alfani. Our local host is a Saudi host-

ess who leads us with enthusiasm to a trendy restaurant that ex-
udes wonderful aromas from its fashionable patio overlooking the
street. As we approach, she explains with a lilt in her voice that
this is a wonderful place where we can all eat *together*, that is, Dr.
Alfani and we three women. "Lately," she confesses, "the PR side
of work has been so demanding that I have just stopped having
people to my house for business. It's so much easier to meet in
restaurants. And people are doing it. They're really doing it. Let
me show you."

At this, the quiet Alfani turns pale. I am as quieted and intrigued by this suggestion as he is threatened, but I do not have
to make a decision for our group, and he does. He really wants
this happy lady to stay happy, but clearly senses she is unwittingly
leading him astray. This is, I'm sure, a first for him. For me, given
the company at hand, it's also a first. Of course, I don't mind if
Dr. Alfani doesn't mind, but he does. More precisely, I'm sure he
is sure we are not allowed to do this. He is a great pauser, and he
pauses now in the wonderful manner in which he invites things to
surface from others.

But our empathetic group prefers to mirror his pain in tripled
silence. None of us stops the lady who proceeds into the open-
doored cafe and directly to the maître d' with her question. I think
of the raiding *matawas* with their arms in flowing robes, waving
mean sticks, and understand fully the issue at hand. Against all
odds, Alfani shouts to halt our lady friend, seeming greatly relieved to reach her and to re-engage her in our roadside huddle.
Leaving all of us feeling like yokels, he says he thinks it is best that
he speak to the maître d'.

We all concur in deference, but I am thinking that the middle
road is probably the one approach bound to lose. When he returns, he tells us that our friend's idea surely is catching on, but will
not suit us here and now, and that he will meet us in this same spot
after dinner. Alfani, the great peacemaker, once again supports
Wahhabi apartheid, as indeed he must. "There is," he announces,

"a lovely room for ladies I understand you will not want to miss."

Such events with the high tea group teach me a lot about the lives that Saudis are living among themselves. They're not the international Arab group that Marc works with, and not the KSU expatriates I worked with either. The Saudis are, of course, grounded here, and issues that other Arabs take on with bravado and that Western expatriates take on with humor are not going away for them. So, I guess, exorbitant public spending, Wahhabi censorship, Saudi intermarriage issues, and the redesign of basic institutions are, for them, not fascinating at all and more like living the angst of *Waiting for Godot.*

It's Beckett who should've written their story from the real inside out, from the place where time stops and where the real future, for all your commitment, is unimaginable. He could've studied the ironic impasse between the raging hormones of fast-circulating petrodollars and the stoic tradition of just sitting quietly in an endless Sufic meditation.

I spend some wonderful months waiting for Godot with Saudis before the sudden end hits, the dreaded, forgotten coming, not of the actually unexpected Godot, but of the very real month of June, the time when everything stops, when we all have to worry about whether to stay or to go. I begin to see it happening. Everybody who can afford it is leaving for the summer, not just those with nine-month contracts. Saudis go to Bahrain and Europe; other Arabs go home, and Americans travel slowly either east or west around the globe, as it's roughly equidistant to home either way. Those whose contracts are not renewed often have to go home on non-stop flights. This last group proves to contain almost all the single female English teachers I first met in Daraiyah last August. Everybody, except for me, seems to be going somewhere.

To Stay or Go_____

A Desert Run

*The absence of shade and the austere aspect
of the place were striking.... When it is windy,
whole hills of sand are carried by the wind
from place to place. When it is calm, as it was
that morning, the silence, uninterrupted by any
movement or sound, is peculiarly striking. That
morning...it was quiet and dull...The air was
hushed, the footfalls...were the only sounds to
be heard....*

I SAVOR SOME old yellowed notes from Tolstoy's *Cossacks*. While
he describes his favorite place, the Caucasus, I feign a momen-
tary beach-like sprawl on a bumpy ridge, an accidental flat niche
in a rising hill (or is it low mountain?) about an hour outside of
Riyadh. I see the same things, more or less, and hear for a bit the
silence too. I have just finished a run with the famous Hash House
Harriers, a British running club that's dropped its slogan and tradition for its Saudi sojourn—"A Drinking Club With a Running
Problem." I've already had my post-run near beer and almost everyone's gone.

Right now I want to stay at least here, this morning, to soak in the quiet and the roughness that always seem beautiful, though it certainly is not. The Harriers open a new part of your brain, give you an inscrutable map to follow to find your group and your victory "beer," but it is more intended to mislead you than lead you, cajoling you through a series of trials, so unfairly spelled the opposite of trails. Once you've lived through it and collaborated with other confused runners who are living through it, you never see that place the same way again. You encounter, as I did, keen-eyed hawks, tranquil lizards, and shady niches, all where you thought there were none, and in my case a serious face-to-face with the country I'm starting to love but am supposed to leave.

What is it the silence muffles for me—everything noisy, crass, and commercial at home that I'm not ready to hear again? My friend will stay too and listen, but after we leave, I probably will not get back again. We won't hear the same thing, because she's been here eight years from England and will be back. She has a different experience racing her feet on Saudi trails, and we won't hear the same quiet either.

Hadji Murad—Metaphor for Saudi Arabia

Meditating on my last experience in the Saudi desert quiet, I think again of Hadji Murad, the favorite character of Tolstoy and of me, who lived in Tolstoy's favorite place, the Caucasus, a sort of Islamic enclave, surrounded by two seas, Persia, Armenia, and Russia itself. In the quiet, I think of Hadji's brutal death at the hands of his enemy tribal warlord, because his death is a silence, and a telling one.

This Chechen who bands with Russia, early man banding with modern man, tribalist banding with a superpower, Muslim banding with Christians, is met with a bureaucratic silence he has never known, so that he breaks his international pact, and challenges his enemy alone, knowing that alone he will almost surely die. He finds and accepts that he cannot reach beyond his fate, that the milieu is the message, that collusion with the superpowers is a poison to the tribal track. Because of this association, he has foregone networks of local strength and loyalty, and lost focus.

When he does die against Shamil, his nemesis, we have the greatest silence in literature: the silence of his loss, the silent "no reply" of the Russians, of his non-anthropomorphic God, and the silence of his acceptance of his fate. According to David Herman,[1] Hadji's death is an example, "not of great, but of perfect faith, the grail of acceptance and surrender.... We witness a man who knew the answer; we witness him knowing the answer. And that is all." He can only have victory, even in defeat, because he accepts his moral imperative totally. In the "glorification of struggle" he is necessarily an epic hero.

I find myself meditating on all of this because, as I see it, Hadji *is* Saudi Arabia, the grand old man who will rise or fall steady in his own truth, and therefore win either way. Saudi Arabia represents another age, but it seems willing to struggle with modernity. It battles with discipline, inside and out, yet is still refining its ethic. The Kingdom finds itself, like Hadji, alone in all the world on its particular moral plane, and this tenacious hold on honor is where the epic story is found. It fascinates me, and I fear to see what the next chapter holds.

The Hadji/Saudi Arabia metaphor helps me understand why I care about this place and why I'm unsure about leaving. I feel that I'm living an important piece of history, in a vulnerable experiment that can be tipped easily. Any of us might serve to help the Kingdom hold its ground *and* mature.

My friend is back, and we leave with her driver for town. She heard hoot owls. I like this, and take it as a good sign. They're a symbol of wisdom, exactly what I need. I heard pure silence, and wish I could put it in a box and take it home.

---

1. In "Khadzhi-Murat's Silence," *Slavic Review,* Spring 2005.

In Motion

When I get home, Marc is standing in wait with a document in his hand. "Mom, what about this release sheet?" He calls this a greeting, as he waves a bureaucratic paper at me, refusing to sit down or even for me to sit down. "Let's see it. Marc, this is in Arabic. I have no idea what it says."

"Mo-om." He's whining just a little. "You're supposed to know about this. You need to have everything on this sheet signed off before we can leave Riyadh. Didn't you have one?"

"No. I never saw it. Where did you get it?"

"They're all over the place. Everybody who's still here has it. Do you realize just about everybody's gone and we haven't started to get signatures on this thing yet?"

"I'm sorry. I really didn't know. But you're right. I figured out that everybody's gone or leaving. I've just been so busy, and I never get to the Women's College to my mailbox anymore. Nobody on this U.N. project is leaving. They're mostly Saudis. Nobody over there is talking about leaving right now. I guess it never occurred to them that you and I would have to go."

"Well, we're supposed to be out of here. Let's read your contract for the employment dates."

"Okay, but how do we read this release sheet if it's in Arabic? Do you know anything about it? I see spots for signatures, but it looks impossible, tons of signatures to get, and we don't know who to get them from."

"I know some of them. The second one is the Women's Library."

"I've never even found the Women's Library! I've never been there. How in the world do I get a signature from there?"

"I don't know, but you have to prove you don't have any books out."

He finally lets me slump into a chair, and kindly brings me a gentle tea. I need something more like sedation. With a little study and some help from neighbors, I do find out, however, what I need to do. I need to leave per my contract in a week or two and there are eight agencies I need release signatures from before I can leave. Of course, the bigger question is whether to leave for just the summer or forever.

I tell Alfani that I have to be released to work this bureaucratic situation full-time, and he agrees. But at the end of the next week, I have only two signatures. No matter what I say to people or how ideal I've been as an employee or resident, most will not sign. How did my colleagues do it? I cannot figure out how other people got their go-ahead and are actually now long gone. Finally, I ask Marc to take the sheet around and see if he can figure out how to get eight signatures. I decide that, while he's afoot, I'll finish last things and say goodbye to a few people.

A Few Goodbyes

Two of my former sociology students at the Women's College want me to visit their homes before leaving. They prove to live in interesting, very different places. One is Huda, the newlywed, and her husband comes to pick me up. They live downtown too, but in an old, poor area, where the streets are still unpaved, lumpy, muddy, and dusty, so narrow and winding I'm sure I could never find my way back alone. This is the old Arabia people imagine in the West, and I am intrigued to know someone who still lives not so unlike her forbears.

Huda and her husband are fresh-faced young adults who are starting out. I pause to remember my first apartment as a newlywed, which does not in its own way seem to have been much. My newlywed days were in a modern setting, but in barely one room, somehow dominated by the refrigerator and a central view of a parking lot. Huda's building is a thick mud-walled structure with almost no windows. It has a cave-like feeling inside that is homey for me, because we sit close together in a part that is lighted, where I'm actually cozy on an extra-thick maroon-colored Oriental rug.

Most of the floors are gray concrete and the walls rough like stucco walls in Arizona. I see no furniture per se at all.

Huda lives in a floor world more than any Saudis I know. I help her cook a bit in the dark, windowless kitchen, where the kitchen floor is meticulous and set with grilling equipment on which we squat and produce fabulous charred lamb. She also has, resting squarely on the concrete floor, a samovar like the exquisite ones that decorate the best hotels. That means lots of tea and I am tea-addicted after a mere nine months. We eat and talk together on the living room carpet after setting down a large white sheet, the Saudi equivalent of "setting the table," and we get to finger all the food and share without utensils, which tastes better and leaves us feeling more like old friends than new ones.

Huda is happy to be married and proud of her trousseau. She shows me each thing they have collected for their life, bringing much out of closets. She goes through each nightgown lingerie set, so we can see them all. There are black ones, bright red ones, and one white one, all very lacy and French-looking. She insists I say which one I prefer until I finally say the white one. Though I refuse to accept it as a gift, three days later the exquisite bedroom gown arrives in a bag her husband leaves with Marc while I am at work. I imagine that to return it would be impolite, so I send her a satin slipper and peignoir set. For me a trade is fun for both of us, but I know Saudis are giddy about this kind of one-way gifting.

There is a certain Third-World gift economy afloat here that has nothing to do with the values of Western capitalism. Just as many American immigrants must sometimes wait a decade to return to their countries of origin because they will be expected to bring thirty gifts for thirty relatives all costing a certain minimum of hundreds of dollars, so the Saudis are dedicated to sharing their wealth on a regular basis. This is problematic for me, as I'm unsure about returning to favorite restaurants that never bill me, etc. Apparently, there is a large scale basis on which non-capitalist economies successfully increase the flow of goods by doing this kind of thing continuously, and it provides a highly social way for people to give and take more than they otherwise would.

I realize I had little time to get to know any of my students this year, and I am thankful for Huda, who also has interesting perspectives on sociology.

I stop by Daraiyah to say goodbye to my last English teacher friend to leave Riyadh. She enjoyed her year, but feels it was hard to get to know Saudis, saying she never made friends with even one. At this, I make a bet with her that I can introduce her to the first Saudi woman I see walking on the green with the success of their becoming friends. We stroll out and do just that, earning me a free last dinner at the Women's Restaurant, where our new Saudi friend joins us and invites my American friend to dine with her at her home the next night.

I feel less successful in my positive social views after dinner, though. We go to the Daraiyah indoor pool for a women's night swim, only to see a beautiful Saudi girl jump into the pool wearing more clothing as she jumps than I have ever seen anyone wear anywhere in winter. Her head, arms, legs, and neck are completely covered, and not in clinging rubbery material that would have the positive effect of a wet suit.

I know this is the traditional swimming outfit, but my friend and I are still aghast, in a room that will not allow any men at all, to see the discomfort of this young lady. She swims quite as long as we do though and seems acclimated to the style du jour. I recall the old beach party photographs of the American twenties in which both men and women look silly in their swimming get-ups. Still, even those old outfits left more room for real swimming.

I visit, as well, Nazira, my other sociology student who lives with her family on the outskirts of the other side of town. I have never been there before and feel glamorous being picked up by her driver. Nazira's family lives in a large, expensive house very different from Huda's home. It's massive, two floors, full of huge rooms and huge furniture, which nonetheless is placed out of the way in each room, always leaving lots of open, carpeted space for floor time.

I meet, contrary to the experiences of many male expatriates I know, her father and her brothers in what I would call the den and later eat in a very formal dining room with her mother and sisters. This family of six is bright, educated, and communicative, and we have long interesting conversations at every meeting point, in halls, in the kitchen, and even in the den with the whole family together. Late at night, their driver takes me home, and I realize how like my own family they are, except that they have a cat. I have learned to fear cats in Riyadh, where the only ones I see, in the city parks, are wild ones that truly look unwell, untamed, and menacing. They stop me from sitting in the parks at all, so I'm now becoming prejudiced against cats. Nazira's cat, Abdu, though, is soft, fluffy, and loved.

The Unavoidable End

All these buddies help me forget my departure crisis, which has only grown as each of my few remaining days elapses. While I wing around, trying to avoid the paperwork, which seems undoable, Marc catches me with a firm jerk again, as I enter the front door. "Sit down, Mom. I have something really important to tell you, and I'm not sure it's good." The last time he brought up this release sheet he wouldn't let me sit down. This time he insists I sit down, so I do. He's convinced me of the gravity of the moment, and frankly, I'm afraid to have this talk.

"Did you have trouble getting all the signatures, Marc? I'm sorry I asked you to do this. Do you have a better idea now of how I can do it myself?"

"Mom, you're not going to get signatures or a release. I was in the personnel department for both colleges, and…well…they don't want you to go!"

"What? This is impossible. They can't not want me to go. I have a perfect right to go." At this point I hear the voices of brothers and sisters who opposed my working here at all, saying how unthinkable it is to go to any country that takes your passport from you. I now hope their point does not come into play. I realize that I have little control of entering and exiting a country without my passport, which Personnel took and held upon my arrival nine months ago.

"You have an appointment tomorrow morning with the head of Personnel. Here's his name. I don't know what to tell you, but things are fixed so that all the agencies on this list know *not* to sign off on your release." We hug each other, eat more than usual, discuss strategies, and I show up in the morning as soon as the head of Personnel does.

Personnel is the scary department for me, the place where so many colleagues have been fired, also the place where I was required to set the terms of my contract after I first arrived. That contract was quite a shock, as all negotiating was done in Arabic, and I knew none; also just because it was being done here, where I have so little recourse, compared with in the U.S., where I'd have had a chance to decide what to accept and what to reject.

The building is coldly marble, glassy. I pass by the pay center where last September I received my first fat envelope of fresh paper riyals, warm from having just been counted by a bill-counting machine on a shelf of stacks of money. This all has a Big Brother effect on me that is eating away at my presence of mind. I hope to not see anyone I know, since I feel almost unable to speak. I decide I'll just put this hapless release document on the head of Personnel's desk, look up, and see if he says anything.

At this moment my whole world flips again, as it has so many times this year, as it did when I met Dr. Al Mani, when the young man walked me home from the payroll office, and when Dr. Alfani praised my lectures and introduced me to the U.N. and the high tea group. At this moment I almost bump into Dr. Talhami, Director of Personnel, who stops everything upon seeing me and beams grandly. "Oh, Dr. Talhami, *Asalam Alaikum*. There seems to be a problem with this release sheet...."

"Please let me interrupt you to sit down," he gestures. "It's early and I'm sure you want some breakfast. Oh, here are some things coming in the door now. Do Americans prefer coffee to tea? We have both here." He begins to set up a plate of pastries, cheese, and fruit for me, and seems earnest about the idea of coffee, which looks great. He hands me my passport and the release sheet with eight red stampings on it. "Of course, your papers are in order for your travel now. You know, though, we don't want to let you go. Your year here has been extraordinary. I wanted to get you here so we can talk about your raise and your project with Dr. Alfani, not just pass forms around."

These words and actions, which sweep me off my shaky feet, are just a prelude to a long, flowery, speech in favor of my signing a continuing contract immediately, after which I would receive release from Saudi Arabia for a three-month break. I am hungry, interested, honored, relieved, and run a gamut of sudden positive feelings all at once. "This is wonderful to know and to hear." I pause. "I do have another problem, however, that seems hard to solve. I need to get my son into Al Manarat High School. He's been out of school all year, and I can't do that again."

At this, Dr. Talhami continues to try to sound reassuring, but he cannot personally give permission for Marc for school. He tries to make it sound likely, but I hear an uncertainty that I feel I must deal with as a mature adult and real parent, something I feel I have reneged on this year. The correct words come out of my mouth that are not the words inside of me. "Thank you, but I cannot return, then. It is too bad. We will leave now as soon as we get flights. If you find a different answer to this school issue, will you let me know before we leave?"

And so my fortunes twist again, sending me to the phone to reach a travel agent, while I am in an awful state over leaving a country I do not want to leave, with a son Saudi Arabia is responsible for over-educating, such that I take home a man in the guise of a kid, who will probably never be happy in any school again.

Unfortunately, even if we take the next available flight, we may not have the three days in Europe I've planned as a minimum trip on the way home. All expatriates perseverate on the topic of where they will travel on their way home, since transport home is paid and it's easy to add stops along the way. I've, however, eaten up most of my travel time already. At home relatives are waiting for us to join them on a prescheduled cruise, and we have just a few days left to meet their schedule.

I call our agent for tickets, and he reminds that I am the plebian on the bottom of a huge list of thousands who all want to leave right now. We are to stay packed for the next few days, so that if tickets are somehow located, we can spring forth at the sound of the ringing phone and show up by taxi at the airport in half an hour. So we prep everything and I repack my Wedgwood china, each piece in a towel again, as I did for the trip coming here. I give away my extravagant plants and lamps, clean everything and turn in all required keys, etc., and we listen for the phone, for me both an exciting sound and a dreaded one.

How can I wake up tomorrow in Europe, next week in Montgomery? Who will remind me to pray, in song no less? What cars will stop for me to cross, because I am a woman, swathed in gown and scarves? Will I ever eat warm bread from fiery medieval ovens again? I can't seem to stop the questions that are filling my mind while we wait. I don't go to Daraiyah to say goodbye to Saudi colleagues, because I am bad at goodbyes. I call instead, and have finished that somehow. Questions keep drowning my brain like high waves, so that I'm in a nervous stupor when the phone does ring.

"Okay. Yes. We're packed. All right, Saudi Air has our tickets. Bye.— Marc, put on your pants. We're going right now." At this, he replies from his bedroom in the back, "What pants?"

"What do you mean, 'What pants?' The ones you wore on our

way here." This demand brings him front and center, holding up the pants he wore last year.

"You don't mean these," he says, displaying a pair so tiny next to his grown body that they look like they belong to a preschooler.

"Oh, God! We'll have to take you as is. Bring your stuff and toss those pants." Upon the moment we are out the door and to the corner for a taxi. At the airport, I can't dispel the insane notion that my books confiscated by security guards last August are still lurking somewhere, or do I just feel I'm visiting their graveyard? Either way I'm not happy to be reminded of them and to return home without them.

As we board and settle, Marc and I have the closest thing to an argument ever. I need to get the upper hand and do what I must to regain my position as parent, after a year as escorted "princess." "I can't really go all the way back to Montgomery," he says. "Mohammed Zubi wants me to go to Turkey with him for June, and stay with his family, but he can meet us in Amsterdam. Then, I've got a chance to go to Egypt with the Zimindars...." I have to interrupt him and do it sharply to end all discussion on this subject, though I'd rather do it kindly, because I appreciate how hard it is for him to leave too.

"Marc, I'm sorry, but you are not a young adult. You're just an American boy, now on your way home to Alabama. That's it. I cannot let you travel with your friends. We're going home." He tries then immediately to impress me with the thousands in cash in his wallet, a normal gesture in this affluent cash society.

"I have the money," he assures, "and I have more. I've worked out the finances." But this dream is too late for him, as are some of my own. "My dearie, I really am sorry, but we have new commitments now. We have to go home together. You have to be just a kid for the next few years." He doesn't answer. He's always been a good kid, and in this moment he's a real man. We don't talk about this disappointment again.

I've never been anywhere in my life except the U.S. and Saudi Arabia, so our plane change in Paris is fascinating. The old Charles De Gaulle Airport is alluring with its ornate ceiling designs and the echoing of footfalls and voices, lots of languages in a polyglot blur, not to mention the deep, nasal French I love, humming from all sides. My problem is, as usual, the fourteen-year-old by my side, who seems, after having been asked to relinquish adult rights for a few years, to have sprung instantly back into belligerent adolescence.

Granted, he had no time to change his clothes before our sudden departure from Riyadh, but at this point it would help if he'd remove his Palestinian *kuffiya*. It would also help if he'd let me buy him some shoes from an airport shop to replace his sandals. His look is a bit arresting for the Charles de Gaulle crowd. Despite ongoing Palestinian terrorist attacks of late, like any teenager, he stubbornly wears the uniform of his peers, in this case a Yassar Arafat look-alike outfit of white *thobe*, brown sandals and a menacingly arrogant *kuffiya*. Arafat always threw the sides of his black-and-white-checked scarf backwards in a style imitative of Marlon Brando's greasy side hair in *The Wild One*. Would Marc consider wearing it in the regular droopy style of some other Arab? No. This Arafat look is *in* in Riyadh.

Unfortunately, we do need to sit down, which proves the most excruciating moment of the entire year abroad. While most have the great difficulty of finding any two seats free together, our attempt to sit down causes eight people to leave the area and give us an entire bench that seats six. Though I smile at everyone who passes, no one is interested in sitting with us. These are the moments in parenting when you know you really love your kid. I never tell him how tempted I am to sit somewhere else myself.

Our destination is Holland for three days, where in nearby Zelham, Germany I can buy the famous Neinhaus Montessori equipment direct at the factory to save for a future school. In Amsterdam, I see I have friends, when we hotfoot it to a department store for new clothes. It proves a Saturday night right before closing time for the rest of the weekend, and Marc's new pants require altering. In the spirit of diplomacy for which the Dutch are so famous, they convince us to remain in the locked-up store after hours until we can get Marc refitted and ready to move back into the Western world.

With no ability to resist the fast and forward flow of time, we find ourselves cast back into Montgomery, feeling that it's all too soon and maybe too much. When we look at each other, I see we have the same unsettled look in our eyes. There's a lot to miss, and we both have culture shock–culture shock coming home. The sameness of things American, the singularity of language, inelegant women and generally androgynous style, T-shirts and shorts, convenience, convenience, and convenience, no one stopping for tea or even allowing you to inconvenience yourself to make some, pre-packaged processed food, fast food, ads, ads, ads, competition, mobility, and upward mobility are all pressing and boring.

Under my arm I see, however, that Tolstoy is still with me, full of the same complaints about Moscow and Petersburg, and dying to escape again to the Caucasus. "Peace of mind," he reminds, "destroys the soul." Thank you, Leo, for standing by me wherever I stay or go. Next to this favorite of my quotations from you, I will now have to add one more, from Kahlil Gibran, Lebanese-American immigrant, active in Arab-American affairs. On "Love" in *The Prophet* he warns not to walk away from what has been offered, lest you "laugh, but not all of your laughter, and cry, but not all of your tears."

Afterword

THESE DAYS AN afterword is irresistible on the subject of a Saudi Arabia long numbed by reluctance to change. In 2009, King Abdullah opened KAUST, the new King Abdullah University of Science and Technology, intended as a true oasis, that is a cultural one, the first coeducational college in the Kingdom, and a campus where female students will not be restricted by the old dress codes and non-driving rules, a haven for assorted academic freedoms, mixed religions, and cultures.

I'm honored to complete this treatise in the same era as the KAUST experiment begins. The King and I seem to be of one mind. At the same time, news releases hint at the six multi-billion dollar eco-cities he has also placed on the drawing board. Both projects are reported to be planned as magnets to pull in an outside world of richness and diversity that has long eluded Arabia. In 1982-83 I saw the same attempt with the new KSU campus to draw the world's best contributors. At that time international employees understood that KSU would not succeed as a cultural magnet because you cannot buy mental, spiritual, and artistic power. KAUST and the eco-cities are different because you can pull spirit with spirit.

This brave difference in approach should be hailed. Muhammad Asad, author of the most insightful English translation and explanation of the *Quran*, in his own tale of leaving the West to adventure across and discover Arabia, exults in the achievements of Islamic society in its first millennium and decries the apathy and decadence too many believers have since fallen into. This bridge of lost time can possibly be rediscovered. In this tired and nervous new millennium, when societal change seems desperately needed across the Middle East, we should look for it wherever we think we can find it. Since it came from these deserts once before, it is not impossible that it will again.

What would Tolstoy, as author of the definitive literary statement, *War and Peace,* see in the Saudi challenge today? His tale of Russians defending themselves against Napoleon is neither practical nor essentially patriotic. His treatment of the subject discouraged historians, politicians, and the power elite by subjugating facts, figures, idolized leaders, historical theory, and national pride to a more potent message. It was really the emerging middle society, says Tolstoy's biographer Henri Troyat, that exulted in the pageantry of life that defines *War and Peace.* And the message they understood is still understandable.

What moves men is history itself, the interplay of each man, class, reality and issue upon all the others. We need not fear a particular state of government, leader, movement, or even tradition; as life is its own force played out through every man and every thing. All that counts is the humanity now, each moment in the present, for none of us will supersede destiny.

In the world of *inshallah,* Tolstoy's point should be well taken. For all the new forces modernity provides, we are still in the hands of an outside force, unable to predict or properly plan. Something eternal emerges in *War and Peace* as in the moment, and that is the role of each stone, star, creature, and human playing its own part its own way. Though America and Saudi Arabia diminish in power, wealth, and tradition, they, like every other country, will each still find and play a crucial role. It's just that there are no answers. There is, for Tolstoy and the Saudis alike, only submission.

Marc and Me

School for Marc in Montgomery proved unthinkably narrow. I was forced to send him for two years to high school in Austin with relatives, where he was able to take advanced classes and Greek and Latin from an Oxford scholar. Before he left me in Montgomery, he entertained our group there with his ready pocketful of vocabulary cards, at first for Gaelic and later Swahili. Wherever we all went, he made us play word games, and we all learned at least a little. I was thankful for the accidental immersion in Arabic that opened him to a world of foreign language.

He also became a Muslim, as did I, something else we could never have imagined before our sojourn. After two semesters of Friday afternoon absences for *Jumma* prayers in Austin, however, Marc's principal told him he'd not be granted enough hours to graduate his senior year, despite honors classes, straight A's, and teacher permission to leave campus for worship. He then dropped out of high school and joined me in California, where he studied Chinese at a community college, passed the GED and went on to the Defense Language Institute in Korean, several degrees, including one in law, one in Korean language from a Korean university, and another in labor relations. He runs a university department in labor relations now in Alabama and is married to a Korean. All his shoes stay on his front porch, and he drinks a lot of tea and speaks Korean at home.

I came home and married my friend in Alabama, the one who originally suggested my Saudi job. He also suggested this book and edited it as if it were his own. In the meantime we resettled in his home state of California, where I worked as a principal of a progressive Los Angeles coed Muslim school and copy editor and staff writer for *The Minaret* magazine. I worked in Montessori also, finally settling into college teaching of English with a favorite emphasis on introducing and relishing the works of Leo Tolstoy.

Glossary

abaya   a light women's cloak

abla   female teacher

Adhan   the call to prayer, a public song

arak   sweet fruit mash smoked in hookahs

Asalam alaikum   Peace be unto you (common greeting)

Baba   Daddy

Collea al Binet   Women's College

dullah   coffee pot

Eid   holiday celebrating the end of Ramadan

entee   you are (masculine)

fulus   money

Hadith   stories about the Prophet

Hajji   *one* who has completed the Haj (pilgrimage to Mecca)

halas   stop

hijab   proper covering for women in public

Hijazi   Arabic accent from the Hijaz or western Saudi Arabia

hene   here

hubbs   bread

ilyaum   today

Inshallah   God willing

Jumma   Prayer, Friday weekly mosque prayer

kuffiya   men's scarf

Kam fulus?   How much money (does it cost)?

Maghrib   sunset prayer

maharam   a lady's escort

ma salama with peace (common goodbye)

matawa moral police

min fudluk please

mush mushkillah no problem

niqab women's face veil

qahwa coffee

salam peace

Salat any one of five daily prescribed prayers

shawarma shaved meat sandwich wrap

shokran thank you

souk outdoor market

tayib okay, all right

thobe men's traditional dress, similar to a cassock

Ummah the community in Islam

wadi desert streambed that's usually dry

Wahhabi ultra-conservative sect of Islam founded by al-Wahhab in Arabia

walimi feast, banquet

yassar, yamin, alatul left, right, straight ahead

Recommended Reading

Al-Turki, Sally. "Being a Woman in Saudi Arabia: A Personal Perspective," *Saudi-American Forum*, SAF Essay #7. February 20, 2003. *www. Saudi-American-Forum.org.*
  A distinguished American-Saudi, speaking from an on-line forum as the wife of a Saudi and long-term resident of the Kingdom about the balance of traditional and progressive values for men and women in Saudi Arabia today.

Asad, Muhammad. *The Road to Mecca.* Fourth revised edition. Gibraltar: Dar al-Andalus,, 1980.
  The memoir of a European journalist's travels through Arabia in the 1920s, by an author who experiences transformation of his own after profound consideration of the cultural values of Arab life.

Lawrence, T.E. *Seven Pillars of Wisdom.* Garden City, New York: Doubleday, 1935.
  The passionate and poetic memoir of Lawrence of Arabia's experiences in the desert during World War I, helping Arab tribes resist Ottoman control. Lawrence's narrative description of the Arab mind reveals his own quest to understand it.

Reese, Lyn. *Women in the Muslim World—Personalities and Perspectives From the Past.* Berkeley: Women in World History Curriculum, 1998.
  Interesting short cultural readings, including poems, songs, photos, and drawings of women who lived in Islamic culture. This anthology is simple and memorable, celebrating strengths and individuality.

Troyat, Henri. *Tolstoy.* New York: Doubleday, 1967.
  The definitive biography, lending enormous insight, sensitivity, and detail to the study of Tolstoy's genius as a writer and an activist. Troyat is almost as great a biographer as Tolstoy is a story teller.